P9-DCT-863

Que® Quick Reference Series

DOS and BIOS Functions
Quick Reference

Developed by
Que Corporation

Que Corporation

Carmel, Indiana

Library of Congress Catalog Number: 88-63857

ISBN 0-88022-426-6

92 91 90 89   5 4 3 2 1

Interpretation of the printing code: the rightmost double-
digit number is the year of the book's printing; the
rightmost single-digit number, the number of the book's
printing. For example, a printing code of 89-4 shows
that the fourth printing of the book occurred in 1989.

This book is based on the latest BIOS and DOS information available, including DOS 4.0.

Que Quick Reference Series

The *Que Quick Reference Series* is a portable resource of essential microcomputer knowledge. Whether you are a new or experienced user, you can rely on the high-quality information in these convenient guides.

Drawing on the experience of many of Que's best-selling authors, the *Que Quick Reference Series* helps you easily access important program information. Now it's easy to look up often-used commands and functions for 1-2-3, WordPerfect 5, MS-DOS, and dBASE IV, as well as programming information for assembly language, C, and QuickBASIC 4.

Use the *Que Quick Reference Series* as a compact alternative to confusing and complicated traditional documentation.

The *Que Quick Reference Series* also includes these titles:

1-2-3 Quick Reference
Assembly Language Quick Reference
C Quick Reference
dBASE IV Quick Reference
Hard Disk Quick Reference
MS-DOS Quick Reference
QuickBASIC Quick Reference
WordPerfect Quick Reference

Publishing Manager
> Allen L. Wyatt, Sr.

Editors
> Gail S. Burlakoff
> Rebecca Whitney

Editorial Assistant
> Ann K. Taylor

Trademark Acknowledgments
> Que Corporation has made every effort to supply trademark information about company names, products, and services mentioned in this quick reference. Trademarks indicated below were derived from various sources. Que Corporation cannot attest to the accuracy of this information.
>
> EPSON is a trademark of Epson America, Inc.
>
> IBM is a registered trademark of International Business Machines Corporation. IBM PC*jr*, PC XT, PC XT 286, and PS/2 are trademarks of International Business Machines Corporation.

Table of Contents

Introduction

This book is intended as a quick reference to BIOS and DOS functions and their use. Because all BIOS and DOS function calls have the same form, this quick reference does not include examples of the use of individual BIOS and DOS calls.

The information in this quick reference was compiled from the widest available range of sources. Every effort was made to ensure the technical accuracy and time-liness of this information; if you find discrepancies, Que Corporation would be interested in your comments.

Each BIOS and DOS function detailed in this quick reference is listed in ascending hexadecimal numeric order, based on the interrupt, function, and (if needed) subfunction numbers. In addition to a short description of the function and its purpose, the following informa-tion is included:

To Call

The setup of registers before the call to the function

Returns

The setup of registers on return from the function

Comments

Short explanatory comments and suggestions about the function and its use

For DOS functions, the version of DOS in which a function first became available is indicated.

This quick reference is designed to help you by remind-ing you of the purposes and register settings for various DOS and BIOS functions. For more detailed reference material, we recommend the following Que titles:

DOS Programmer's Reference
Using Assembly Language

In the following comprehensive list of BIOS and DOS functions, all numbers are hexadecimal. The BIOS and DOS columns indicate the function's classification and where in this quick reference the function is described. Functions marked with *X* are covered; those marked with # are not.

BIOS	DOS	Int	Func (AH)	Subfunc (AL)	Purpose
#		00			Divide-by-Zero
#		01			Single Step Interrupt
#		02			Non-Maskable
#		03			Breakpoint Interrupt
#		04			Arithmetic Overflow
#		05			Print Screen
#		06, 07			Reserved
#		08			System Timer
#		09			Keyboard
#		0A			Reserved
#		0B			Communications
#		0C			Communications
#		0D			Hard Disk Controller
#		0E			Floppy Disk Management
#		0F			Printer Management
X		10	00		Set Video Mode
X			01		Set Cursor Mode
X			02		Set Cursor Position
X			03		Read Cursor Position and Configuration
X			04		Read Light Pen Position
X			05		Select Active Display Page
X			06		Scroll Window Up
X			07		Scroll Window Down
X			08		Read Character and Attribute
X			09		Write Character and Attribute
X			0A		Write Character at Cursor
X			0B		Set Color Palette
X			0C		Write Graphics Pixel
X			0D		Read Graphics Pixel
X			0E		Write Text in Teletype Mode
X			0F		Get Current Display Mode
X			10		Set Palette Registers
X			11		Character Generator
X			13		Write String
X		11			Get Equipment Status
X		12			Get Memory Size
X		13	00		Reset Floppy Disk System
X			01		Get Floppy Disk System Status
X			02		Read Floppy Disk
X			03		Write Disk Sectors
X			04		Verify Disk Sectors

BIOS	DOS	Int	Func (AH)	Subfunc (AL)	Purpose
X		13	05		Format Disk Track
#			06, 07		Reserved
X			08		Return Disk Drive Parameters
X			09		Initialize Fixed Disk Table
X			0A		Read Long Sector
X			0B		Write Long Sector
X			0C		Seek Cylinder
X			0D		Alternate Disk Reset
#			0E–14		Reserved
X			15		Return DASD Type
X			16		Read Disk Change Line Status
X			17		Set DASD Type for Disk Format
X			18		Set Media Type for Format
X		14	00		Initialize Communications Port
X			01		Write Character to Communications Port
X			02		Read Character from Communications Port
X			03		Request Communications Port Status
X			04		Extended Initialization (PS/2)
X			05		Extended Com Port Control (PS/2)
#		15	00		Turn On Cassette Motor
#			01		Turn Off Cassette Motor
#			02		Read Data Blocks from Cassette Drive
#			03		Write Data Blocks to Cassette Drive
X			0F		Format Unit Periodic Interrupt (PS/2)
X			21		Power-On Self-Test Error Log (PS/2)
X			4F		Keyboard Intercept
X			80		Device Open
X			81		Device Close
X			82		Program Termination
X			83		Event Wait
X			84		Joystick Support
X			85		System Request Key Pressed
X			86		Wait
X			87		Move Block
X			88		Get Extended Memory Size
X			89		Switch Processor to Protected Mode
X			90		Device Busy
X			91		Interrupt Complete
X			C0		Return System-Configuration Parameters
X			C1		Return EBDA Segment Address
X			C2		Pointing Device BIOS Interface
X			C3		Enable/Disable Watchdog Timeout
X			C4		Programmable Option Select
X		16	00		Read Keyboard Character
X			01		Read Keyboard Status
X			02		Return Keyboard Flags
X			05		Write to Keyboard Buffer
X			10		Get Keystroke
X			11		Check Keyboard

BIOS	DOS	Int	Func (AH)	Subfunc (AL)	Purpose
X		16	12		Get Keyboard Status Flags
X		17	00		Write Character to Printer
X			01		Initialize Printer Port
X			02		Request Printer Port Status
#		18			Execute ROM BASIC
X		19			System Warm Boot
X		1A	00		Get Clock Counter
X			01		Set Clock Counter
X			02		Read Real-Time Clock
X			03		Set Real-Time Clock
X			04		Read Date from Real-Time Clock
X			05		Set Date of Real-Time Clock
X			06		Set System Alarm
X			07		Disable Real-Time Clock Alarm
X		1B			Ctrl-Break Handler Address
X		1C			Timer Tick Interrupt
X		1D			Video-Initialization Parameter Table
X		1E			Disk-Initialization Parameter Table
X		1F			Graphics Display Character Bit-Map Table
	X	20			Terminate Program
	X	21	00		Terminate Program
	X		01		Keyboard Input with Echo
	X		02		Display Output
	X		03		Auxiliary Input
	X		04		Auxiliary Output
	X		05		Printer Output
	X		06		Direct Console I/O
	X		07		Direct STDIN Input
	X		08		STDIN Input
	X		09		Display String
	X		0A		Buffered STDIN Input
	X		0B		Check STDIN Status
	X		0C		Clear Buffer and Input
	X		0D		Reset Disk
	X		0E		Select Disk
	X		0F		Open File (FCB)
	X		10		Close File (FCB)
	X		11		Search for First Entry (FCB)
	X		12		Search for Next Entry (FCB)
	X		13		Delete File (FCB)
	X		14		Read Sequential File (FCB)
	X		15		Write Sequential File (FCB)
	X		16		Create File (FCB)
	X		17		Rename File (FCB)
	#		18		Reserved
	X		19		Get Default Drive
	X		1A		Set DTA Address
	X		1B		Get Allocation Table Information
	X		1C		Get Allocation Table Information for Specific Drive

BIOS	DOS	Int	Func (AH)	Subfunc (AL)	Purpose
	#	21	1D–20		Reserved
	X		21		Random File Read (FCB)
	X		22		Random File Write (FCB)
	X		23		Get File Size (FCB)
	X		24		Set Random-Record Field (FCB)
	X		25		Set Interrupt Vector
	X		26		Create PSP
	X		27		Random Block Read (FCB)
	X		28		Random Block Write (FCB)
	X		29		Parse File Name
	X		2A		Get System Date
	X		2B		Set System Date
	X		2C		Get System Time
	X		2D		Set System Time
	X		2E		Set Verify Flag
	X		2F		Get DTA Address
	X		30		Get DOS Version Number
	X		31		Terminate and Stay Resident
	#		32		Reserved
	X		33		Get/Set System Values
	#		34		Reserved
	X		35		Get Interrupt Vector
	X		36		Get Free Disk Space
	#		37		Reserved
	X		38		Get/Set Country Information
	X		39		Create Subdirectory
	X		3A		Remove Subdirectory
	X		3B		Set Directory
	X		3C		Create/Truncate File (handle)
	X		3D		Open File (handle)
	X		3E		Close File (handle)
	X		3F		Read File or Device (handle)
	X		40		Write to File or Device (handle)
	X		41		Delete File
	X		42		Move File Pointer
	X		43		Get/Set File Attributes
	X		44	00	IOCTL: Get Device Information
	X			01	IOCTL: Set Device Information
	X			02	IOCTL: Character Device Read
	X			03	IOCTL: Character Device Write
	X			04	IOCTL: Block Driver Read
	X			05	IOCTL: Block Driver Write
	X			06	IOCTL: Get Input Status
	X			07	IOCTL: Get Output Status
	X			08	IOCTL: Block Device Removable?
	X			09	IOCTL: Block Device Local or Remote?
	X			0A	IOCTL: Handle Local or Remote?
	X			0B	IOCTL: Set Sharing Retry Count

			Func	*Subfunc*	
BIOS	*DOS*	*Int*	*(AH)*	*(AL)*	*Purpose*
	X	21	44	0C	IOCTL: Generic I/O for Handles
	X			0D	IOCTL: Generic I/O for Block Devices
	X			0E	IOCTL: Get Logical Drive Map
	X			0F	IOCTL: Set Logical Drive Map
	X		45		Duplicate Handle
	X		46		Force Duplicate Handle
	X		47		Get Current Directory
	X		48		Allocate Memory
	X		49		Release Memory
	X		4A		Modify Memory Allocation
	X		4B	00	Execute Program (EXEC)
	X			03	Load Overlay
	X		4C		Terminate with Return Code
	X		4D		Get Return Code
	X		4E		Search for First Match
	X		4F		Search for Next Match
	#		50–53		Reserved
	X		54		Get Verify Flag
	#		55		Reserved
	X		56		Rename File
	X		57	00	Get File Date and Time
	X			01	Set File Date and Time
	#		58		Reserved
	X		59		Get Extended Error Information
	X		5A		Create Temporary File
	X		5B		Create File
	X		5C		Set File Access
	#		5D		Reserved
	X		5E	00	Get Machine Name
	X			02	Set Printer Setup
	X			03	Get Printer Setup
	X		5F	02	Get Redirection List Entry
	X			03	Redirect Device
	X			04	Cancel Redirection
	#		60, 61		Reserved
	X		62		Get PSP Address
	X		63	00	Get System Lead Byte Table
	X			01	Set Interim Console Flag
	X			02	Get Interim Console Flag
	#		64		Reserved
	X		65		Get Extended Country Information
	X		66	01	Get Global Code Page
	X			02	Set Global Code Page
	X		67		Set Handle Count
	X		68		Flush Buffer
	#		69–6B		Reserved
	X		6C		Extended Open/Create
	X	22			Terminate Address
	X	23			Ctrl-C Interrupt Vector

BIOS	DOS	Int	Func (AH)	Subfunc (AL)	Purpose
	X	24			Critical-Error Vector
	X	25			Absolute Disk Read
	X	26			Absolute Disk Write
	X	27			Terminate and Stay Resident
	X	2F	01	00	Print Installation Check
	X			01	Print Submit File
	X			02	Print Remove File
	X			03	Print Remove All Files
	X			04	Print Hold Queue/Get Status
	X			05	Print Restart Queue
	#		B7	00	APPEND Installation Check
	#	33			Microsoft Mouse
	#	5C			NETBIOS Interface
	#	67	40		Get EMM Status
	#		41		Get Page Frame Segment
	#		42		Get Number of Pages
	#		43		Get Handle/Allocate Memory
	#		44		Map Memory
	#		45		Release Handle and Memory
	#		46		Get EMM Version
	#		47		Save Mapping Context
	#		48		Restore Mapping Context
	#		49		Reserved
	#		4A		Reserved
	#		4B		Get Number of EMM Handle
	#		4C		Get Pages Owned by Handle
	#		4D		Get Pages for All Handles
	#		4E	00	Get Page Mapping Registers
	#			01	Set Page Mapping Registers
	#			02	Get/Set Page Mapping Registers
	#			03	Get Size of Page Mapping Array
	#		4F		Get/Set Partial Page Map
	#		50		Map/Unmap Multiple Handle Pages
	#		51		Reallocate Pages
	#		53		Get/Set Handle Name
	#		54		Get Handle Directory
	#		55		Alter Page Map and Jump
	#		56		Alter Page Map and Call
	#		57		Move/Exchange Memory Region
	#		58		Get Mappable Physical Address Array
	#		59		Get Expanded Memory Hardware Information
	#		5A		Allocate New Pages
	#		5B		Alternate Page Map Register Set
	#		5C		Prepare Expanded Memory Hardware
	#		5D		Enable/Disable OS/E Function Set
X		70			Real-Time Clock Interrupt

BIOS Functions Reference

The BIOS (Basic Input/Output System) functions are the fundamental level of any PC or compatible computer. BIOS functions embody the basic operations needed for successful use of the computer's hardware resources.

Common Data Areas and Tables

This section contains descriptive tables for data areas and other information referred to throughout the BIOS function reference.

Table 1. Video Display Modes

Mode	Type	Adapter	Resolution	Box	Char	Colors
00h	Text	CGA[3]	320 x 200	8 x 8	40 x 25	16
		EGA[2,3]	320 x 350	8 x 14	40 x 25	16
		MCGA	320 x 400	8 x 16	40 x 25	16
		VGA[1]	360 x 400	9 x 16	40 x 25	16
01h	Text	CGA	320 x 200	8 x 8	40 x 25	16
		EGA[2]	320 x 350	8 x 14	40 x 25	16
		MCGA	320 x 400	8 x 16	40 x 25	16
		VGA[1]	360 x 400	9 x 16	40 x 25	16
02h	Text	CGA[3]	640 x 200	8 x 8	80 x 25	16
		EGA[2,3]	640 x 350	8 x 14	80 x 25	16
		MCGA	640 x 400	8 x 16	80 x 25	16
		VGA[1]	720 x 400	9 x 16	80 x 25	16
03h	Text	CGA	640 x 200	8 x 8	80 x 25	16
		EGA[2]	640 x 350	8 x 14	80 x 25	16
		MCGA	640 x 400	8 x 16	80 x 25	16
		VGA[1]	720 x 400	9 x 16	80 x 25	16
04h	Graph	CGA/EGA/ MCGA/VGA	320 x 200	8 x 8	40 x 25	4
05h	Graph	CGA/EGA[3]	320 x 200	8 x 8	40 x 25	4
		MCGA/VGA	320 x 200	8 x 8	40 x 25	4
06h	Graph	CGA/EGA/ MCGA/VGA	640 x 200	8 x 8	80 x 25	2
07h	Text	MDA/EGA	720 x 350	9 x 14	80 x 25	Mono
		VGA[1]	720 x 400	9 x 16	80 x 25	Mono
08h	Graph	PC*jr*	160 x 200	8 x 8	20 x 25	16
09h	Graph	PC*jr*	320 x 200	8 x 8	40 x 25	16
0Ah	Graph	PC*jr*	640 x 200	8 x 8	80 x 25	4
0Bh	——RESERVED——					
0Ch	——RESERVED——					

Mode	Type	Adapter	Resolution	Box	Char	Colors
0Dh	Graph	EGA/VGA	320 x 200	8 x 8	40 x 25	16
0Eh	Graph	EGA/VGA	640 x 200	8 x 8	80 x 25	16
0Fh	Graph	EGA/VGA	640 x 350	8 x 14	80 x 25	Mono
10h	Graph	EGA/VGA	640 x 350	8 x 14	80 x 25	16
11h	Graph	MCGA/VGA	640 x 480	8 x 16	80 x 30	2
12h	Graph	VGA	640 x 480	8 x 16	80 x 30	16
13h	Graph	MCGA/VGA	320 x 200	8 x 8	40 x 25	256

[1] Enhanced VGA mode; otherwise, the VGA can emulate either CGA or EGA characteristics for this mode.

[2] EGA mode when connected to an enhanced color display; otherwise, emulates CGA characteristics for this mode.

[3] Denotes shades of gray.

Table 2. Equipment Status Word

Bit	Meaning
0	Disk drive installed = 1
1	Math coprocessor installed = 1
2–3	System board RAM
	00 = 16K
	01 = 32K
	10 = 48K
	11 = 64K
2	Pointing device installed = 1 (PS/2)
3	Not used (PS/2)
4–5	Initial video mode
	01 = 40 x 25 color
	10 = 80 x 25 color
	11 = 80 x 25 mono
6–7	Number of disk drives (if bit 0 = 1)
	00 = 1 drive attached
	01 = 2 drives attached
	10 = 3 drives attached
	11 = 4 drives attached
8	Not used
9–11	Number of serial cards attached
12	Game adapter installed = 1
12	Not used (PS/2)
13	Not used
13	Internal modem installed = 1 (PS/2)
14–15	Number of printers attached

Table 3. Disk Controller Status Bits

76543210	Meaning
. . . . 1	Illegal command to driver
. . . . . . 1 .	Address mark not found (bad sector)
. . . . . . 1 1	Write-protected disk
. . . . . 1 . .	Requested sector not found
. . . . . 1 1 .	Diskette change line active
. . . . 1 . . .	DMA overrun
. . . . 1 . . 1	DMA attempt across 64K boundary
. . . . 1 1 . .	Invalid media
. . . 1	CRC error on disk read
. . 1	Controller error
. 1	Seek failure
1	Disk time out (drive not ready)

Table 4. Port Status Bits

76543210	Meaning
. . . . 1	Data ready
. . . . . . 1 .	Overrun error
. . . . . 1 . .	Parity error
. . . . 1 . . .	Framing error
. . . 1	Break detected
. . 1	Transmit holding register (THR) empty
. 1	Transmit shift register (TSR) empty
1	Time out

Table 5. Modem Status Bits

76543210	Meaning
. . . . 1	Change in Clear to Send (CTS) status
. . . . . . 1 .	Change in Data Set Ready (DSR) status
. . . . . 1 . .	Trailing edge ring indicator
. . . . 1 . . .	Change in receive line signal
. . . 1	Clear to Send (CTS)
. . 1	Data Set Ready (DSR)
. 1	Ring Indicator
1	Receive line signal detected

Table 6. Cassette Services Return Codes

Code	Meaning
00h	Invalid command
01h	CRC error
02h	Data transitions lost
03h	No data located on tape
04h	Data not found (PC*jr* only)
86h	No cassette port available

Table 7. The Global Descriptor Table

Offset	Description
00h	Dummy (Set to zero)
08h	GDT data segment location (Set to zero)
10h	Source GDT pointer
18h	Target GDT pointer
20h	Pointer to BIOS code segment, initialized to zero. BIOS will use this area to create the protected-mode code segment.
28h	Pointer to BIOS stack segment, initialized to zero. BIOS will use this area to create the protected mode stack segment.

Source/Target GDT Layout

Offset	Description
00h	Segment limit
02h	24-bit segment physical address
05h	Data access rights (set to 93h)
06h	Reserved word (must be zero)

Table 8. Print Status Bits

76543210	Meaning
.......1	Time-out
.....xx.	Unused
....1...	I/O error
...1....	Printer selected
..1.....	Out of paper
.1......	Acknowledged
1.......	Printer not busy

The BIOS Functions

Int 10/00

Set Video Mode—sets display mode used by video adapter

To Call

AH	00h
AL	Display mode (see table 1)

Returns

Nothing

Comments

Sets video mode, clears screen, and selects video adapter (if more than one is present). To prevent screen-clear on EGA, MCGA, and VGA systems, set bit 7 of AL to 1.

Int 10/01

Set Cursor Type—used to set height of video cursor

To Call

AH	01h
CH	Starting (top) scan line in bits 0–4
CL	Ending (bottom) scan line in bits 0–4

Returns

Nothing

Comments

Sets the type of text-mode cursor by specifying cursor's starting and ending scan lines, starting with line 0. For monochrome modes, default starting scan line is 0Bh and ending scan line is 0Ch. For color modes, default starting scan line is 06h and ending scan line is 07h.

Int 10/02

Set Cursor Position

To Call

AH	02h
BH	Page number (0 for graphics modes)
DH	Row
DL	Column

Returns

Nothing

Comments

Used to position cursor at a specific location. Positions are defined relative to the upper left corner (0,0) when screen is in text mode. The lower left corner is (79,24) in 80 x 25 text mode, (39,24) in 40 x 25 modes.

Pages	*Modes*	*Adapters*
0–7	00h, 01h	CGA, EGA, MCGA, VGA
0–3	02h, 03h	CGA
0–7	02h, 03h	EGA, MCGA, VGA
0	07h	MDA
0–7	07h	EGA, VGA

Int 10/03

Read Cursor Position and Configuration

To Call

AH	03h
BH	Page number

Returns

BH	Video page number
CH	Starting scan line for cursor
CL	Ending scan line for cursor
DH	Row
DL	Column

Comments

Gets starting and ending cursor scan lines and current cursor position. Returns the same values used to position the cursor with Int 10/02.

Int 10/04

Read Light Pen Position

To Call

AH	04h

Returns

AH	0, Light pen not down/not triggered
	1, Light pen down/triggered
BX	Pixel column (0 through 319 or 0 through 639, depending on mode)
CH	Pixel row (0 through 199)
CX	Pixel row (0–nnn, depending on mode)
DH	Character row (0 through 24)
DL	Character column (0 through 79 or 0 through 39, depending on mode)

Comments

Reads light pen's status and position. Returns valid information only if the light pen has been triggered (AH = 1). The light pen returns a vertical position accurate to only two lines. Horizontal accuracy is no better than two (320 pixels per line) or four pixels (640 pixels per line). PS/2™ systems (MCGA or VGA) do not support the light pen (AH will always return 00h).

Int 10/05

Select Active Display Page

To Call
AH	05h
AL	Page number selected (see table in *Comments*)

Returns
Nothing

Comments
Selects the active (displayed) video page. Works with the CGA, MCGA, EGA, or VGA adapters but cannot be used with monochrome adapters, which have only one display page of memory. Valid page numbers are

Pages	*Modes*	*Adapters*
0–7	00h, 01h	CGA, EGA, MCGA, VGA
0–3	02h, 03h	CGA
0–7	02h, 03h	EGA, MCGA, VGA
0–7	07h, 0Dh	EGA, VGA
0–3	0Eh	EGA, VGA
0–1	0Fh, 10h	EGA, VGA

Int 10/06

Scroll Window Up

To Call
AH	06h
AL	Number of lines to scroll
BH	Attribute used for blanked area
CH	Row, upper left corner
CL	Column, upper left corner
DH	Row, lower right corner
DL	Column, lower right corner

Returns

Nothing

Comments

Clears a window with a specified attribute, or scrolls the window up a specified number of lines. All lines in the window are moved up and blank lines are added at the bottom. To clear a window, set AL either to 0 or to a value greater than the number of lines in the window.

Int 10/07

Scroll Window Down

To Call

AH	07h
AL	Number of lines to scroll
BH	Attribute used for blanked area
CH	Row, upper left corner
CL	Column, upper left corner
DH	Row, lower right corner
DL	Column, lower right corner

Returns

Nothing

Comments

Functions exactly the same as Int 10/06, except that the lines in the window are moved down.

Int 10/08

Read Character and Attribute

To Call

AH	08h
BH	Display page

Returns

AH	Attribute byte
AL	ASCII character

Comments

Reads the character and attribute bytes (for a specified display page) at the cursor's current position.

Int 10/09

Write Character and Attribute

To Call

AH	09h
AL	ASCII character
BH	Display page
BL	Attribute byte of character in AL
CX	Number of characters to write

Returns

Nothing

Comments

Writes ASCII-character and attribute bytes at the cursor position on a specified display page. This function does not change the cursor position.

Writes as many as 65,536 characters in text mode. As the function writes characters, it wraps lines. In graphics mode, the function goes only to the end of the current line and the video attribute byte in BL determines the color of the character written. If bit 7 is set, the value in BL is XORed with the background color when the character is displayed.

Int 10/0A

Write Character at Cursor

To Call

AH	0Ah
AL	ASCII character
BH	Display page number
BL	Color of character in AL (graphics modes)
CX	Number of characters to write

Returns

Nothing

Comments

Operates exactly the same as Int 10/09, except that the display attributes are not changed in text mode. See *Comments* under Int 10/09 for more information.

Int 10/0B

Set Color Palette

To Call

AH	0Bh
BH	Color palette ID being set
	0, BL has background and border color
	1, BL has palette color
BL	Color value to be used for that color ID

Returns

Nothing

Comments

This function selects or sets the contents of the color palette and works only for medium-resolution graphics displays. The function has no direct effect on memory; it affects the way the 6845 CRT controller interprets video memory. In text mode, this function sets border color. The valid color palettes for this function are

Palette	Pixel	Color
0	0	Same as background
	1	Green
	2	Red
	3	Brown
1	0	Same as background
	1	Cyan
	2	Magenta
	3	White

Int 10/0C

Write Graphics Pixel—writes single pixel to the screen at a specified coordinate

To Call

AH	0Ch
AL	Color value
BH	Page number
CX	Pixel column number
DX	Pixel row number

Returns
Nothing

Comments
In medium-resolution modes, the effect of this function depends on the palette in use. If bit 7 of AL is 1, the new color is XORed with the current pixel. Refer to table 1 for details on screen limits by mode.

Int 10/0D

Read Graphics Pixel

To Call

AH	0Dh
BH	Page number
CX	Pixel column number
DX	Pixel row number

Returns

AL	Color value

Comments

Gets the value of the pixel at the specified graphics coordinates. Refer to table 1 for details on the addressing limits of various video modes. Refer to Int 10/0C for the valid page numbers that can be set in BH.

Int 10/0E

Write Text in Teletype Mode

To Call

AH	0Eh
AL	ASCII character
BH	Display page (alpha modes)
BL	Foreground color (graphics modes)

Returns

Nothing

Comments

Writes text to the screen with limited character processing. The function interprets the ASCII codes for bell (07h), backspace (08h), carriage return (0Dh), and line feed (0Ah). After the write, the cursor moves to the next character position.

To work on PC BIOS ROMs dated 4/24/81 and

10/19/81, the BH register *must* point to the currently displayed page.

Int 10/0F

Get Current Display Mode

To Call
AH   0Fh

Returns
AH	Number of columns on-screen
AL	Display mode (see table 1)
BH	Active display page

Comments
Gets the video controller's display mode, including the
number of columns and the current display page.

Int 10/10

Set Palette Registers—controls (based on subfunction
loaded in AL) operations on the color-palette registers
within EGA/VGA video controllers

To Call
AH	10h
AL	00h, Set palette register
BH	Color value
BL	Palette register to set
AL	01h, Set border color register
BH	Color value
AL	02h, Set all registers and border
ES:DX	Pointer to 17-byte color list

AL	03h, Toggle blink/intensity (EGA only)
BL	00h = Enable intensity
	01h = Enable blinking
AL	07h, Read palette register (PS/2)
BL	Palette register to read (0–15)
AL	08h, Read overscan register (PS/2)
AL	09h, Read palette registers/border (PS/2)
ES:DX	Pointer to 17-byte table for values
AL	10h, Set individual color register
BX	Color register to set
CH	Green value to set
CL	Blue value to set
DH	Red value to set
AL	12h, Set block of color registers
BX	First color register to set
CX	Number of color registers to set
ES:DX	Pointer to color values
AL	13h, Select color page
BL	00h, Select paging mode
BH	Paging mode
	00h = 4 register blocks of 64 registers
	01h = 16 register blocks of 16 registers
AL	13h, Select color page
BL	01h, Select page
BH	Page number
	00–03h for 64-register blocks
	00–0Fh for 16-register blocks
AL	15h, Read color register (PS/2)
BX	Color register to read
AL	17h, Read block of color registers
BX	First color register to read
CX	Number of color registers to read
ES:DX	Pointer to buffer to hold color register values
AL	1Ah, Read color page state

AL	1Bh, Sum color values to gray shades
BX	First color register to sum
CX	Number of color registers to sum

Returns

Subfunctions 07h and 08h

| BH | Value read |

Subfunction 09h

| ES:DX | Pointer to 17-byte table |

Subfunction 15h

CH	Green value read
CL	Blue value read
DH	Red value read

Subfunction 17h

| ES:DX | Pointer to color table |

Subfunction 1Ah

| BL | Current paging mode |
| CX | Current page |

Comments

On the PC*jr*™, MCGA, EGA, and VGA display systems, this function controls the correspondence of colors to pixel values. This function is an extension to the BIOS, applicable to EGA/VGA display systems. A detailed explanation of this function is beyond the scope of this quick reference.

Int 10/11

Character Generator—supports (based on subfunction loaded in AL) graphics character-generator functions

To Call

AL	00h, User alpha load
BH	Number of bytes per character
BL	Block to load

CX	Count to store
DX	Character offset into table
ES:BP	Pointer to user table
AL	01h, ROM monochrome set
BL	Block to load
AL	02h, ROM 8 x 8 double dot
BL	Block to load
AL	03h, Set block specifier
BL	Character-generator block selection
AL	10h, User alpha load
BH	Number of bytes per character
BL	Block to load
CX	Count to store
DX	Character offset into table
ES:BP	Pointer to user table
AL	11h, ROM monochrome set
BL	Block to load
AL	12h, ROM 8 x 8 double dot
BL	Block to load
AL	20h, Set user characters pointer at 1Fh
ES:BP	Pointer to user table
AL	21h, Set user characters pointer at 43h
BL	Row specifier
CX	Bytes per character
ES:BP	Pointer to user table
AL	22h, ROM 8 x 14 set
BL	Row specifier
AL	23h, ROM 8 x 8 double dot
BL	Row specifier
AL	30h, System information
BH	Font pointer

Returns

Varies by subfunction

Comments

This function is an extension to the BIOS, applicable to EGA/VGA display systems. A detailed explanation is beyond the scope of this quick reference.

Int 10/13

Write String

To Call

AH	13h
AL	Write mode (see table in *Comments*)
BH	Video page
BL	Attribute (write modes 0 and 1)
CX	Length of string
DH	Row at which to write string
DL	Column at which to write string
ES:BP	Pointer to string

Returns

Nothing

Comments

Available only on PC XT™ s with BIOS dates of 1/10/86 or later, on the PC/AT, and on the PS/2. Writes a string of characters to the current display. The designated string can have either embedded or global character attributes. The mode (AL) is specified as follows:

Mode	Comments
0	Attribute in BL. String is characters only. Cursor not updated.
1	Attribute in BL. String is characters only. Cursor updated.
2	String alternates characters and attributes. Cursor not updated.
3	String alternates characters and attributes. Cursor updated.

Int 11

Get Equipment Status

To Call

Nothing

Returns

AX   Equipment status word (see table 2)

Comments

During the booting process, the hardware status byte is set to indicate what equipment is attached to the computer. As indicated in table 2, the meaning of the different bits varies according to computer type. To determine which type of machine you are using, check the computer's signature byte at address FFFF:FFFE.

Int 12

Get Memory Size

To Call

Nothing

Returns

AX   Number of 1K memory blocks

Comments

Returns the number of *contiguous* 1K memory blocks found during start-up memory checks of the system.

Int 13/00

Reset Floppy Disk System

To Call

AH	00h
DL	Drive number (0 based)
	bit 7 = 0 for diskette; 1 for fixed disk

Returns

Carry flag clear if successful

Carry flag set if error

AH	Return code (refer to table 3)

Comments

Resets the floppy disk in preparation for I/O by setting a reset flag in the disk controller, thus forcing the drive to pull the heads to track 0 for the next disk operation.

Int 13/01

Get Floppy Disk System Status

To Call

AH	01h

Returns

AH	Status byte (see table 3)

Comments

The status of the controller is set after each disk operation. With this function, your program can get the status of the disk as of the most recent disk operation.

Int 13/02

Read Floppy Disk

To Call

AH	02h
AL	Number of sectors to transfer (1 through 9)
ES:BX	Pointer to user's disk buffer
CH	Track number (0 through 39)
CL	Sector number (1 through 9)
DH	Head number (0 or 1)
DL	Drive number (0 through 3)

Returns

Carry flag clear if successful

AL	Number of sectors transferred

Carry flag set if error

AH	Status byte (see table 3)

Comments

Transfers one or more sectors from the floppy disk into memory. All input parameters should be checked carefully before you issue a call for service; passing an invalid value can lead to unpredictable results.

Int 13/03

Write Disk Sectors

To Call

AH	03h
AL	Number of sectors to transfer (1 through 9)
ES:BX	Pointer to user's disk buffer
CH	Track number (0 through 39)
CL	Sector number (1 through 9)
DH	Head number (0 or 1)
DL	Drive number (0 through 3)

Returns

Carry flag clear if successful

AH	0
AL	Number of sectors transferred

Carry flag set if error

AH	Status byte (see table 3)

Comments

Writes one or more sectors from memory to the floppy disk. Except for the disk drive number, values are not checked for validity. Passing an invalid value may lead to unpredictable results.

Int 13/04

Verify Disk Sectors

To Call

AH	04h
AL	Number of sectors to verify (1 through 9)
CH	Track number (0 through 39)
CL	Sector number (1 through 9)
DH	Head number (0 or 1)
DL	Drive number (0 through 3)

Returns

Carry flag clear if successful

AH	0

Carry flag set if error

AH	Status byte (see table 3)

Comments

Disk verification causes the system to read the data in the designated sector or sectors and to check its computed CRC (Cyclic Redundancy Check) against data stored on the disk.

Int 13/05

Format Disk Track

To Call

AH	05h
ES:BX	Pointer to track address field list
CH	Track number
DH	Head number
DL	Drive number

Returns

AH	Return code (see table 3)

Comments

Formats a disk track by initializing the disk address fields and data sectors. The disk-formatting operation is controlled by the track address field list (ES:BX). The table is laid out as a series of 4-byte entries (one for each sector on the track), with each entry as follows:

Byte Offset	Meaning
00h	Track number
01h	Head number
02h	Sector number
03h	Size code

The following table shows allowable size codes; the entries are laid out in the order in which the sectors will appear on disk. This order need not be sequential.

Size Code	Bytes per Sector
0	128
1	256
2	512
3	1024

Formatting a disk track is only one part of formatting a whole disk. For further information on using this function, see *Using Assembly Language*.

Int 13/08

Return Disk Drive Parameters

To Call

AH	08h
DL	Drive number (0 based)
	bit 7 = 0 for diskette; 1 for fixed disk

Returns

Carry flag clear if successful

CH	Number of tracks per side
CL	Number of sectors per track
DH	Number of sides
DL	Number of consecutive drives attached
ES:DI	Pointer to 11-byte diskette parameter table
BL	Valid drive-type value from CMOS
	01h = 5.25", 360K, 40 track
	02h = 5.25", 1.2M, 80 track
	03h = 3.5", 720K, 80 track
	04h = 3.6", 1.44M, 80 track

Carry flag set if error

AH	Error status (see table 3)

Comments

Available only on the PC/AT (BIOS dated after 1/10/84) and the PS/2. Allows you to check the characteristics of the disk in the designated drive. On return, the table pointed to by ES:DI has the following format:

Offset	Meaning
00h	First specify byte
01h	Second specify byte
02h	Number of timer ticks before turning off drive motor
03h	Number of bytes per sector
	00h = 128 02h = 512
	01h = 256 03h = 1024
04h	Sectors per track
05h	Gap length
06h	Data length

Offset	Meaning
07h	Gap length for format
08h	Fill byte for format
09h	Head settle time in milliseconds
0Ah	Motor startup time in 1/8ths seconds

Int 13/09

Initialize Fixed Disk Table—sets (to their default values) the values in the specified fixed disk table

To Call

AH	09h
DL	Fixed disk drive number

Returns

Carry flag clear if successful

AH	0

Carry flag set if error

AH	Status byte (see table 3)

Comments

Use this function, *which is available only on the PC/AT and PS/2 and works only on hard disks,* to set the hard disk drive's physical parameters. Drive numbers are from a special series of numbers for fixed disks (80h corresponds to the first disk, 81h to the second, etc.). Using an out-of-range disk drive number will lead to unpredictable results.

Initialization information for the drive is taken from the fixed disk parameter tables. Interrupt vector 41h points to the table for disk 1; vector 46h points to the table for disk 2. If a reference is made for any other disk, the function returns an *invalid command* status byte in AH.

Int 13/0A

Read Long Sector

To Call

AH	0Ah
AL	Number of sectors
ES:BX	Pointer to data buffer
CH	Track
CL	Sector
DH	Head number
DL	Fixed disk drive number

Returns

Carry flag clear if successful

AH   0

Carry flag set if error

AH   Status byte (see table 3)

Comments

Available only on the PC/AT and works only on hard disks. Reads long sectors (standard sectors with 4 bytes of error-correcting code). Drive numbers are from a special series of numbers for hard disks (80h corresponds to the first disk, 81h to the second, etc.).

The following table gives valid parameter ranges for this function. *Note that the track number is a 10-bit number stored with the 2 high-order bits in CL and the 8 low-order bits in CH.* The sector is a 6-bit number stored in bits 0 through 5 of CL.

Register	Parameter	Valid range
AL	# sectors	1 through 121
CH/CL	Track	0 through 1023
CL	Sector	1 through 17
DH	Head	0 through 15
DL	Drive	80h, 81h, etc.

Int 13/0B

Write Long Sector

To Call

AH	0Bh
AL	Number of sectors
ES:BX	Pointer to data buffer
CH	Track
CL	Sector
DH	Head number
DL	Fixed disk drive number

Returns

Carry flag clear if successful
AH   0

Carry flag set if error
AH   Status byte (see table 3)

Comments

Available only on the PC/AT and works only on hard disks. Long sectors are standard sectors that contain four bytes of error-correcting code. Drive numbers are from a special series of numbers for fixed disks (80h is the first disk, 81h the second, etc.). An out-of-range drive number will lead to unpredictable results.

Int 13/0C

Seek Cylinder

To Call

AH	0Ch
CH	Low-order track
CL	High-order track
DH	Head number
DL	Fixed disk drive number

Returns

Carry flag clear if successful

AH 0

Carry flag set if error

AH Status byte (see table 3)

Comments

Available only on the PC/AT and works only on hard disks. Moves the read/write heads to a specified cylinder. Drive numbers are from a special series of numbers for fixed disks (80h corresponds to the first disk, 81h to the second, etc.). Using an out-of-range disk drive number will lead to unpredictable results.

Int 13/0D

Alternate Disk Reset

To Call

AH 0Dh

DL Fixed disk drive number

Returns

Carry flag clear if successful

AH 0

Carry flag set if error

AH Status byte (see table 3)

Comments

Available only on the PC/AT and works only on hard disks. Drive numbers are from a special series of numbers for fixed disks (80h corresponds to the first disk, 81h to the second, etc.). Using an out-of-range disk drive number will lead to unpredictable results. This function is identical to Int 13/00.

Int 13/15

Return DASD (Direct Access Storage Device) Type

To Call

AH	15h
DL	Drive number

Returns

Carry flag clear if successful

AH	DASD type of drive
CX:DX	Number of fixed disk sectors

Carry flag set if error

AH	Status byte (see table 3)

Comments

Available only on the PC XT (BIOS dated 1/10/86 or later), PC XT 286™, PC/AT, or PS/2. Uses standard BIOS drive numbers (0 = A:, 1 = B:, etc.) or fixed disk numbers (80h = first drive, 81h = second drive, etc.).

Used to determine whether Int 13/16 can be used to test for disk changing. The following table lists valid return codes. The value returned in CX:DX is valid only if the DASD type (AH) is 3.

Code	DASD Type
0	Drive requested is not available
1	Drive present, cannot detect disk change
2	Drive present, can detect disk change
3	Fixed disk

Int 13/16

Read Disk Change Line Status

To Call

AH	16h
DL	Drive number

Returns

Carry flag clear
AH   00, Disk not changed

Carry flag set
AH   00, Error
            06, Disk changed

Comments

Use this function, *which is available only on the PC XT (BIOS dated 1/10/86 or later), PC XT 286, PC/AT, or PS/2,* to determine whether the disk in a drive has been changed or removed. This function uses either standard drive numbers (0 = A:, 1 = B:, etc.) or fixed-disk-only numbers (80h = first drive, 81h = second drive, etc.).

Int 13/17

Set DASD Type for Disk Format

To Call

AH   17h
AL   DASD format type (see table in *Comments*)
DL   Drive number (0 based)

Returns

Nothing

Comments

Available only on the PC XT (BIOS dated 1/10/86 or later), PC XT 286, PC/AT, or PS/2. Must be called before formatting a disk. Informs BIOS of the DASD type for formatting operations. A list of the disk types that can be formatted on the PC/AT system follows:

Type	Meaning
1	Formatting 320/360K disk in 320/360K drive
2	Formatting 320/360K disk in 1.2M drive
3	Formatting 1.2M disk in 1.2M drive

Int 13/18

Set Media Type for Format

To Call

AH	18h
CH	Number of tracks (0 based)
CL	Sectors per track
DL	Drive number (0 based); bit 7 = 0 for a diskette, 1 for fixed disk

Returns

Carry flag clear if successful

ES:DI	Pointer to 11-byte parameter table (refer to *Comments* section of Int 13/08.)

Carry flag set if error

AH	Return code

Comments

Available only on the PC/AT (BIOS dated after 11/15/86), PC XT (BIOS dated after 1/10/86), PC XT 286, and the PS/2. Specifies to BIOS the type of media it can expect to find in the disk drive when formatting a track with Int 13/05. When using this function, note the use of CH and CL to specify the track and sector information. See Int 13/0A for more information.

Int 14/00

Initialize Communications Port

To Call

AH	00h
AL	Initialization parameter
DX	Port number (0=COM1, 1=COM2); (2=COM3, 3=COM4 on PC/AT)

Returns

AH   Port status

AL   Modem status

Comments

Used to initialize a serial port (DX). Specify how the port should be initialized (AL) using the following:

Bits 7,6,5 *Baud Rate*	*Bits 4,3* *Parity*	*Bit 2* *Stop Bits*	*Bits 1,0* *Word Length*
000 = 110 baud	X0=none	0=1 bit	10=7 bits
001 = 150 baud	01=odd	1=2 bits	11=8 bits
010 = 300 baud	10=none		
011 = 600 baud	11=even		
100 = 1200 baud			
101 = 2400 baud			
110 = 4800 baud			
111 = 9600 baud			

Int 14/01

Write Character to Communications Port

To Call

AH   01h

AL   Character to write

DX   Port number (0=COM1, 1=COM2);
            (2=COM3, 3=COM4 on PC/AT)

Returns

AH   bit 7 = 0 (no error)

AH   bit 7 = 1 (error); bits 0 through 6 show cause
            of failure (see table 4)

Comments

Writes a character to and returns the status of the specified serial port. Before you call this function, be sure to use Int 14/00 to initialize the port.

Int 14/02

Read Character from Communications Port

To Call

AH	02h
DX	Port number (0=COM1, 1=COM2); (2=COM3, 3=COM4 on PC/AT)

Returns

AH	bit 7 = 0 (no error)
AL	Character
AH	bit 7 = 1 (error); bits 0 through 6 show failure cause (see table 4)

Comments

Reads a character from the specified serial port and returns the port's status. Before calling this function, you must initialize the port.

Int 14/03

Request Communications Port Status

To Call

AH	03h
DX	Port number (0=COM1, 1=COM2); (2=COM3, 3=COM4 on PC/AT)

Returns

AH	Port status (see table 4)
AL	Modem status (see table 5)

Comments

This function, which returns the status of the specified communications port, requests the status without doing additional I/O or affecting the port in any other way.

Int 14/04

Extended Initialization (PS/2)

To Call

AH	04h
AL	Break setting
BH	Parity
BL	Stop bits
CH	Data length
CL	Transmission rate (bps)
DX	Port number (0=COM1, 1=COM2, 2=COM3, 3=COM4)

Returns

AH	Port status (see table 4)
AL	Modem status (see table 5)

Comments

Allows serial port initialization on the PS/2. Possible register settings for this function are

Reg	Meaning	Settings	Meaning
AL	Break	00h	No break
		01h	Break
BH	Parity	00h	No parity
		01h	Odd parity
		02h	Even parity
		03h	Stick parity odd
		04h	Stick parity even
BL	Stop Bits	00h	One stop bit
		01h	Two stop bits (1 1/2 if CH is 00h)
CH	Data Length	00h	5-bit word length
		01h	6-bit word length
		02h	7-bit word length
		03h	8-bit word length
CL	BPS Rate	00h	110 baud
		01h	150 baud
		02h	300 baud
		03h	600 baud

Reg	Meaning	Settings	Meaning
CL	BPS Rate	04h	1200 baud
		05h	2400 baud
		06h	4800 baud
		07h	9600 baud
		08h	19200 baud

Int 14/05

Extended Communications Port Control (PS/2)

To Call
AH	05h
AL	Read or write modem control register (00h = read, 01h = write)
BL	Modem control register (if AL = 01h; see table in *Comments*)
DX	Port number (0=COM1, 1=COM2, 2=COM3, 3=COM4)

Returns
AH	Port status (see table 4)
AL	Modem status (see table 5)
BL	Modem control register (see table in *Comments*)

Comments

Allows reading or writing the modem control register associated with the desired RS-232 port. The bits in BL are defined in the following table:

76543210	Meaning
.......1	Data Terminal Ready (DTR)
......1.	Request to Send (RTS)
.....1..	Out1
....1...	Out2
...1....	Loopback test
111.....	Reserved

Int 15/0F

Format Unit Periodic Interrupt

To Call

AH	0Fh
AL	Phase code
	00h, Reserved
	01h, Surface analysis
	02h, Formatting

Returns

Carry flag set, end of formatting or scanning

Carry flag clear, continue formatting or scanning

Comments

Available only on the PS/2. Used to gain control after formatting or scanning each disk cylinder. At that time, the format routine will call this interrupt.

If this function is invoked from any machine other than a PS/2, the carry flag will be set and AH will contain 80h (PC and PC*jr*) or 86h (all others) on return.

Int 15/21

Power-On Self-Test Error Log

To Call

AH	21h
AL	00h, Read POST error log
	01h, Write error code to POST error log
BX	POST error code if AL=01h
BH	Device code
BL	Device error

Returns

If *reading* POST error log (AL = 0)

Carry flag clear if successful

AH	00h
BX	Number of POST error codes stored
ES:DI	Pointer to POST error log

Carry flag set if error

AH	80h, (PC*jr* and PC)
AH	86h, (all others)

If *writing* error code to POST error log (AL = 1)

Carry flag clear if successful

AH	00h

Carry flag set if error

AH	01h, POST error log full
AH	80h, (PC*jr* and PC)
AH	86h, (all others including PS/2 Model 30)

Comments

Used by the POST on PS/2 machines (except Model 30) to write information to the internal error log, or by diagnostic routines to gain information about errors detected during the POST. The use of this error log is beyond the scope of this quick reference.

Int 15/4F

Keyboard Intercept

To Call

AH	4Fh
Carry flag set	
AL	Keyboard scan code

Returns

PC, PC*jr*:

Carry flag set, AH=80h

PC XT BIOS 11/08/82, PC/AT BIOS 1/10/84:
Carry flag set, AH=86h

All Others:
Carry flag set
AL   New scan code

Carry flag clear
AL   Original scan code

Comments

Available only on the PC/AT (BIOS dated after 1/10/84),
PC XT (BIOS dated after 11/8/82), PC XT 286, and PS/
2. Called by Int 09; normally returns the scan code in the
AL register with the carry flag set. Purpose of the
routine is to translate scan codes for the keyboard
interrupt. If function returns with the carry flag clear, Int
09 will ignore the character.

Int 15/80

Device Open

To Call

AH	80h
BX	Device ID
CX	Process ID

Returns

Carry flag set if error
AH   80h (PC, PC*jr*)
AH   86h (PC XT with BIOS 11/8/82)

Comments

Available only on the PC/AT, PC XT (BIOS dated after
11/8/82), PC XT 286, and PS/2. Intended for use in
rudimentary multitasking operations, this function is
beyond the scope of this quick reference.

Int 15/81

Device Close

To Call

AH	81h
BX	Device ID
CX	Process ID

Returns

Carry flag set if error

AH	80h (PC, PC*jr*)
AH	86h (PC XT with BIOS 11/8/82)

Comments

Available only on the PC/AT, PC XT (BIOS dated after 11/8/82), PC XT 286, and PS/2. Intended for use in rudimentary multitasking operations, this function is beyond the scope of this quick reference.

Int 15/82

Program Termination—used to terminate a process

To Call

AH	82h
BX	Device ID

Returns

Carry flag set if error

AH	80h (PC, PC*jr*)
AH	86h (PC XT with BIOS 11/8/82)

Comments

Available only on the PC/AT, PC XT (BIOS dated after 11/8/82), PC XT 286, and PS/2. Intended for use in rudimentary multitasking operations, this function is beyond the scope of this quick reference.

Int 15/83

Event Wait

To Call
AH	83h
AL	00h, Set interval
CX:DX	Microseconds until posting
ES:BX	Pointer to byte with high-order bit set as soon as possible after end of interval
AL	01h, Cancel set interval (PS/2)

Returns
Carry flag clear if successful

Carry flag set if error
AH	80h, (PC)
AH	86h, (PC XT, PC/AT)

Comments
This function—*available only on PC/AT (BIOS dated after 1/10/84) and PS/2*—does not work with the PS/2 Model 30. Intended for rudimentary multitasking operations, it is beyond the scope of this quick reference.

Int 15/84

Joystick Support

To Call
AH	84h
DX	00h, Read switch settings
	01h, Read joystick position

Returns
PC, PC*jr*:
Carry flag set, AH = 80h

PC XT BIOS 11/08/82:
   Carry flag set, AH = 86h

All others:
   DX   00h (on calling)
            AL = Switch settings (bits 4 through 7)
            Carry flag set if error

   DX   01h (on calling)
            AX = A(X) value
            BX = A(Y) value
            CX = B(X) value
            DX = B(Y) value

Comments

Controls joystick operation on all *except* the PC, PC*jr*, and early PC XT (BIOS dated 11/08/82). If invoked on these computers, the carry flag is set and AH returns the error code: either 80h or 86h (PC XT).

Int 15/85

System Request Key Pressed

To Call

   AH   85h

Returns

PC, PC*jr*:
   Carry flag set, AH = 80h

PX XT BIOS 11/08/82:
   Carry flag set, AH = 86h

All Others:
   AL   00h, Key pressed
            01h, Key released

Comments

BIOS calls this function whenever the System Request

key (Alt-Print Screen) is pressed or released. *Only the more recent versions of BIOS support this function,* which is accessible only from keyboards with a System Request key. If a computer's BIOS does not support this function, the carry flag will be set and AH will contain either 80h or 86h (early PC XT) on return.

Int 15/86

Wait

To Call
AH	86h
CX,DX	Time before return in microseconds (accurate to within 976 microseconds)

Returns
PC, PC*jr*:
  Carry flag set, AH = 80h

PC XT:
  Carry flag set, AH = 86h

All Others:
  Carry flag set (Wait in progress)
  Carry flag clear (Successful wait)

Comments
Works only on the PC/AT and PS/2. Designed to be used within operating system software for setting up system waits, it is not intended for use by applications programs.

Int 15/87

Move Block

To Call

AH	87h
CX	Word count of storage to be moved
ES:SI	Pointer to Global Descriptor Table

Returns

PC, PC*jr*:
  Carry flag set, AH = 80h

PC XT, PS/2 Model 30:
  Carry flag set, AH = 86h

All Others:
  Carry flag clear, Zero flag set
    AH   00h, Operation successful

  Carry flag set, Zero flag clear
            Operation failed
    AH   01h, RAM parity error
            02h, Other exception occurred
            03h, Gate address line 20h failed

Comments

Allows transfer of data blocks (up to 64K) to and from extended memory on 80286/80386 systems. Transfers are done without interruption in protected mode. The Global Descriptor Table (ES:SI) is shown in table 7.

Int 15/88

Get Extended Memory Size

To Call

AH	88h

Returns

PC, PC*jr*:
  Carry flag set, AH = 80h

PC XT, PS/2 Model 30:

  Carry flag set, AH = 86h

All Others:

  AX   Contiguous 1K blocks of memory beginning
              at 100000h

Comments

Returns the amount of memory determined available by
POST checks above address 100000h. Notice that this
function is available only for machines using either the
80286 or 80386 microprocessor.

Int 15/89

Switch Processor to Protected Mode

To Call

  AH   89h
  BL   IRQ0 interrupt vector offset
  BH   IRQ8 interrupt vector offset
  ES:SI   Pointer to Global Descriptor Table (GDT)
  CX   Offset into protected mode CS to jump to

Returns

Carry flag clear if successful

Carry flag set if error

Comments

Switches the processor to protected mode so that it can
access extended memory and take advantage of
protected mode instructions. To use this function, set
up the Global Descriptor Table (GDT) for the call
(refer to table 7). While in use, normal BIOS functions
are not available.

Int 15/90

Device Busy

To Call

AH	90h
AL	Device type code
ES:BX	Pointer to network control block if waiting for a network

Returns

PC, PC*jr*:

Carry flag set, AH = 80h

PC XT BIOS (11/08/82):

Carry flag set, AH = 86h

All Others:

Carry flag set (Minimum wait satisfied)

Carry flag clear (Wait not satisfied)

Comments

This function is used to tell the operating system that a program is about to wait for a device. Typically used in designing or developing multitasking software, this function is not meant for use by applications programmers. The following table lists the type codes passed to the routine in AL:

AL	*Type Code*
00h	Disk timeout
01h	Diskette timeout
02h	Keyboard (no timeout)
03h	Pointing device (timeout)
80h	Network (no timeout)
FCh	Fixed disk reset (PS/2)
FDh	Diskette drive motor start (timeout)
FEh	Printer (timeout)

Int 15/91

Interrupt Complete

To Call
AH   91h

Returns
PC, PC*jr*:
  Carry flag set, AH = 80h

PC XT BIOS (11/08/82):
  Carry flag set, AH = 86h

All Others:
  AL   Type code

Comments
Int 15/91 is not meant to be called by applications programmers; it is intended to be used internally by the operating system, or to develop multitasking systems. BIOS uses this function to report that the device interrupt is complete, according to the type codes listed in the *Comments* section of Int 15/90.

Int 15/C0

Return System-Configuration Parameters

To Call
AH   C0h

Returns
PC, PC*jr*:
  Carry flag set, AH = 80h

PC XT BIOS (11/08/82), PC/AT BIOS (1/10/84):
  Carry flag set, AH = 86h

All Others:
:   **ES:BX**   Pointer to system-descriptor table in ROM

Comments

The ROM system-descriptor table contains useful
information about the system. The following table
shows the meaning of the entries:

Offset	Meaning
00h	Byte count of data that follows (minimum 8)
02h	Model byte
03h	Submodel byte
04h	BIOS revision level (00 = 1st release)
05h	Feature information (see following table)
06–09h	Reserved

76543210	Meaning
. . . . x	Reserved
. . . . . . 0 .	PC bus I/O channel
. . . . . . 1 .	Micro channel architecture
. . . . . 1 . .	EBDA allocated
. . . . 1 . . .	Wait for external event is supported
. . . 1	Keyboard intercept called by Int 09
. . 1	Real-time clock present
. 1	Second interrupt chip present
1	DMA channel 3 used by hard disk BIOS

The model byte contained at offset 02h of the system-
descriptor table should be same as the system ID byte
(stored at FFFF:FFFE). The submodel byte (offset 03h)
can be used for additional system identification.

Int 15/C1

Return EBDA Segment Address

To Call

:   **AH**   C1h

Returns

PC, PC*jr*:

Carry flag set, AH = 80h

PC XT, PC/AT:

Carry flag set, AH = 86h

PS/2:

Carry flag set (Unsuccessful)

Carry flag clear (Successful)
ES   Extended BIOS data-area segment address

Comments

Used to determine the segment address of the extended
BIOS data area (EBDA). The EBDA is used internally
by BIOS on the PS/2. It is allocated by the POST
routines and resides at the top of the user memory area.

Int 15/C2

Pointing Device BIOS Interface

To Call

AH	C2h
AL	00h, Enable/disable pointing device
BH	00h, Enable
	01h, Disable
AL	01h, Reset pointing device
AL	02h, Set sample rate
AL	03h, Set resolution
AL	04h, Read device type
AL	05h, Pointing device interface initialization
AL	06h, Extended commands
AL	07h, Pointing device far call initialization

Returns

    PC, PC*jr*:
      Carry flag set, AH = 80h

    PC XT, PC/AT:
      Carry flag set, AH = 86h

    PS/2:
      Carry flag clear if successful
        Other registers vary by subfunction (see *Comments*)

      Carry flag set if error
        AH   01h, Invalid function call
                  02h, Invalid input
                  03h, Interface error
                  04h, Resend
                  05h, No far call installed

Comments

    Works only on the PS/2. Designed to interface pointing devices (such as a mouse or digitizer) to DOS. This function is beyond the scope of this quick reference.

Int 15/C3

    Enable/Disable Watchdog Timeout

To Call

    AH   C3h
    AL   00h, Disable watchdog timeout
             01h, Enable watchdog timeout
    BX   Watchdog timer count (1 through 255)

Returns

    PC, PC*jr*:
      Carry flag set, AH = 80h

    PC XT, PC/AT, PS/2 Model 30:
      Carry flag set, AH = 86h

PS/2:
  Carry flag clear if successful
  Carry flag set if error

Comments

Used to enable or disable the watchdog timer available with PS/2s that use the 80286 or 80386. The watchdog timer uses timer channel 3 and is tied to the IRQ0 line. When IRQ0 is active for more than one cycle of the channel 0 timer (main system timer), the watchdog timer count is decremented. When the watchdog timer reaches 0, a non-maskable interrupt (NMI) is generated.

Int 15/C4

Programmable Option Select—provides access to PS/2 system programmable registers on option boards

To Call

AH	C4h
AL	00h, Get base POS adapter register address
	01h, Enable slot for setup
	02h, Adapter enable

Returns

PC, PC*jr*:
  Carry flag set, AH = 80h

PC XT, PC/AT, PS/2 Model 30:
  Carry flag set, AH = 86h

PS/2:
  Carry flag clear if successful
| DL | POS adapter register address (function 0) |
| BL | Slot number (function 1) |

  Carry flag set if error

Comments

The Programmable Option Select (POS), available on PS/2 models that use the 80286 and 80386, eliminates the need for system-board and adapter switches. The switches are replaced by programmable registers accessible through this function.

Int 16/00

Read Keyboard Character

To Call

    AH   00h

Returns

    AH   Keyboard scan code
    AL   ASCII character code

Comments

Waits for and reads a single character from the keyboard buffer and returns the character and its scan code. The keyboard buffer usually is located at 0040:001A.

Int 16/01

Read Keyboard Status

To Call

    AH   01h

Returns

Zero flag clear (Key waiting)
    AH   Scan code
    AL   ASCII character

Zero flag set (No key waiting)

Comments

If a keystroke is ready, this function clears the zero flag and returns the keystroke's ASCII code and the keyboard scan code. If no keystroke is waiting to be processed, the function sets the zero flag and returns.

Int 16/02

Return Keyboard Flags

To Call

AH   02h

Returns

AL   ROM BIOS keyboard flags byte

Comments

Returns the status of keyboard toggles and Shift keys from the BIOS status register kept in memory location 0000:0417h. The following table shows the meaning of the bits in the AL register on return from the function:

76543210	Meaning
. . . . 1	Right Shift key depressed
. . . . . . 1 .	Left Shift key depressed
. . . . . 1 . .	Ctrl key depressed
. . . . 1 . . .	Alt key depressed
. . . 1	Scroll Lock enabled
. . 1	Num Lock enabled
. 1	Caps Lock enabled
1	Insert key toggled

Int 16/05

Write to Keyboard Buffer

To Call

AH	05h
CH	Scan code
CL	Character

Returns

AL	01h if buffer is full

Comments

Works only on PC/ATs and PS/2s with enhanced keyboards. Stores a character in the buffer of an enhanced keyboard.

Int 16/10

Get Keystroke

To Call

AH	10h

Returns

AH	Scan code
AL	Character

Comments

Works only on PC/ATs and PS/2s with enhanced keyboards. Allows recognition of similar keys (see Int 16/12 for a table of additional key identifications.)

Int 16/11

Check Keyboard

To Call

AH	11h

Returns

Zero flag clear if keystroke is available

AH   Scan code

AL   Character

Zero flag set if no keystroke is available

Comments

Works only on PC/ATs and PS/2s with enhanced keyboards. Returns a character and scan code if one is available, or returns the zero flag set if not available.

Int 16/12

Get Keyboard Status Flags

To Call

AH   12h

Returns

AL   Status flag 1

AH   Status flag 2

Comments

This function, *which works only on PC/ATs and PS/2s with enhanced keyboards,* is similar to Int 16/02, except that extended information is returned. For the meaning of the status flags see tables 9 and 10.

Table 9. BIOS Keyboard Status Flag 1

76543210	*Meaning*
. . . . 1	Right Shift key depressed
. . . . . . 1 .	Left Shift key depressed
. . . . . 1 . .	Either Ctrl key depressed
. . . . 1 . . .	Either Alt key depressed
. . . 1	Scroll Lock enabled
. . 1	Num Lock enabled
. 1	Caps Lock enabled
1	Insert key toggled

Table 10. BIOS Keyboard Status Flag 2

76543210	Meaning
. . . . 1	Left Ctrl key depressed
. . . . . . 1 .	Left Alt key depressed
. . . . . 1 . .	Right Ctrl key depressed
. . . . 1 . . .	Right Alt key depressed
. . . 1	Scroll Lock depressed
. . 1	Num Lock key depressed
. 1	Caps Lock key depressed
1	SysReq Key depressed

Int 17/00

Write Character to Printer

To Call

AH	00h
AL	Character
DX	Printer number (0 through 2)

Returns

AH	Printer status (see table 8)

Comments

Writes the specified character to the printer port and returns the printer's current status, as shown in table 8.

Int 17/01

Initialize Printer Port

To Call

AH	01h
DX	Printer number (0 through 2)

Returns

AH   Printer status (see table 8)

Comments

Initializes the parallel printer port and returns the port's status. The function outputs the character sequence 08h 0Ch to the printer port. EPSON™ and IBM® printers respond to this sequence by resetting. Other printers may not respond correctly or may exhibit undesirable effects.

Int 17/02

Request Printer Port Status

To Call

AH   02h
DX   Printer number (0 through 2)

Returns

AH   Printer status (see table 8)

Comments

Returns the status of the specified parallel printer port (see table 8). If you are using a PC/AT, PC XT 286, or PS/2, and BIOS determines that the printer is busy (see bit 7 of table 8), BIOS will execute an Int 15/90.

Int 19

System Warm Boot

To Call

Nothing

Returns

Nothing

Comments

Similar to Ctrl-Alt-Del, this function performs a warm boot without losing the present status of memory.

Int 1A/00

Get Clock Counter

To Call

AH	00h

Returns

AL	Midnight flag
CX:DX	Clock count

Comments

Retrieves the system clock counter, which ticks 18.2065 times per second. Zero is equal to midnight.

Int 1A/01

Set Clock Counter

To Call

AH	01h
CX:DX	Clock count

Returns

Nothing

Comments

To set the clock to a particular time, compute the number of ticks you want to represent. Do this by

multiplying by 18.2065 the number of seconds since
midnight for the desired time setting.

Int 1A/02

Read Real-Time Clock

To Call

AH   02h

Returns

Carry flag clear if successful

CH   Hours (BCD)
CL   Minutes (BCD)
DH   Seconds (BCD)
DL   Daylight savings time flag

Carry flag set if error

Comments

This function (*available only on the PC XT 286, PC/AT,
or PS/2*) returns the clock values in BCD (Binary Coded
Decimal). For PC/AT BIOS dated before 6/10/85, DL is
not returned. If the carry flag is set, the clock is not
functioning.

Int 1A/03

Set Real-Time Clock

To Call

AH   03h
CH   Hours (BCD)
CL   Minutes (BCD)
DH   Seconds (BCD)
DL   Daylight savings time

Returns

Nothing

Comments

Available only on the PC XT 286, PC/AT, or PS/2.
Clock values should be set in BCD (Binary Coded
Decimal). DL is coded to indicate whether the clock is
keeping standard time (DL = 0) or daylight savings
time (DL = 1).

═Int 1A/04

Read Date from Real-Time Clock

To Call

AH   04h

Returns

Carry flag clear if successful

CH	Century (BCD)
CL	Year (BCD)
DH	Month (BCD)
DL	Day (BCD)

Carry flag set if error

Comments

This function, *which is available only on the PC XT
286, PC/AT, and PS/2,* returns the clock values in BCD
(Binary Coded Decimal). If the carry flag is set, the
clock is not functioning.

═Int 1A/05

Set Date of Real-Time Clock

To Call

AH	5h
CH	Century (BCD) (19 or 20)
CL	Year (BCD)
DH	Month (BCD)
DL	Day (BCD)

Returns

Nothing

Comments

Available only on the PC XT 286, PC/AT, or PS/2.
Clock values should be set in BCD (Binary Coded
Decimal).

Int 1A/06

Set System Alarm—sets the system alarm timer to
generate an interrupt at a future time

To Call

AH	06h
CH	Hours (BCD)
CL	Minutes (BCD)
DH	Seconds (BCD)

Returns

Carry flag clear if successful

Carry flag set if error

Comments

Available only on the PC XT 286, PC/AT, or PS/2.
Alarm settings must be in BCD (Binary Coded Decimal).

The alarm setting is an offset from the present time.
When time runs out, the system will trigger Int 04
(Arithmetic Overflow). Before you reset an alarm, you

must disable it with Int 1A/07 and set up an interrupt handler to deal with the alarm.

Int 1A/07

Disable Real-Time Clock Alarm

To Call

AH   07h

Returns

Nothing

Comments

This function, *which is available only on the PC XT, PC/AT, or PS/2*, disables the real-time alarm clock. If you have already set the alarm, this function must be called before you can reset it.

Int 1B

Ctrl-Break Handler Address

To Call

Nothing

Returns

Nothing

Comments

Interrupt vector 1Bh contains the address of the Ctrl-Break interrupt handler. Control is transferred to this address when a program is terminated by a Ctrl-Break key sequence.

Int 1C

Timer Tick Interrupt

To Call

Nothing

Returns

Nothing

Comments

Vector 1Ch, the timer tick interrupt called by Int 08, is initialized to point to an IRET instruction. A TSR that needs to be triggered at each clock tick can reset the vector to point to a custom interrupt handler.

Int 1D

Video-Initialization Parameter Table

To Call

Nothing

Returns

Nothing

Comments

Int 1D (which is not a true interrupt) points to a table of initialization parameters for the video controller. Because Int 1D is *not* executable code, this interrupt should not be called by a program.

Int 1E

Disk-Initialization Parameter Table

To Call

Nothing

Returns

Nothing

Comments

Int 1E (which is not a true interrupt) points to the
diskette base table, a table of initialization parameters
for the disk controller. Because Int 1E is *not* executable
code, this interrupt should not be called by a program.

Int 1F

Graphics Display Character Bit-Map Table

To Call

Nothing

Returns

Nothing

Comments

Int 1F (which is not a true interrupt) points to a table of
character bit maps for the graphics mode representa-
tions of ASCII characters 128 to 255. By resetting this
vector, you can create your own characters for use in
CGA graphics modes. Such operations are beyond the
scope of this quick reference.

Int 70

Real-Time Clock Interrupt—called 1,024 times per
second to control periodic and alarm functions

To Call

Nothing

Returns

Nothing

Comments

This function applies only to PC AT, PC XT 286, and PS/2 product lines. (The periodic function is not included on the PS/2 Model 30).

Whenever this interrupt is called, a double-word counter is decremented by 976 microseconds (1/1024 of a second). The initial value of this counter is set by calls to Int 15/83 or 15/86. When the counter reaches a value less than or equal to zero, bit 7 of the designated wait flag is set. For Int 15/83, the wait flag is specified by ES:BX. For Int 15/86, the flag is at 0040:00A0h.

If the real-time clock is activated as an alarm function by a call to Int 1A/06, then when time runs out, Int 4A is called by Int 70 to activate the alarm handler. (The alarm handler must be set up before the call to Int 1A).

DOS Functions Reference

The services offered by DOS cover interrupts in the range of 20–2Fh. Many of these interrupts and their functions are detailed in this section.

Common Data Areas and Tables

The following tables show the layout of both standard and extended File Control Blocks (FCB). These data areas are used in many of the DOS functions.

Table 11. Standard File Control Block

Offset	Length	Meaning & Notes
00h	Byte	Drive number. 0=default, 1=A:, 2=B:, etc.
01h	8 bytes	Left-justified ASCII file name; padded with blanks
09h	3 bytes	Left-justified ASCII file extension; padded with blanks
0Ch	Word	Current block number
0Eh	Word	Record size; default of 80h bytes with DOS *open* or *create* functions
10h	Dword	File size
14h	Word	Date created/updated
16h	Word	Time created/updated
18h	8 bytes	Reserved
20h	byte	Current record number
21h	Dword	Random record number (if record size is less than 64 bytes, only 3 bytes used)

Table 12. An Extended File Control Block

Offset	Length	Meaning & Notes
00h	Word	FFh—signals that this is an extended FCB
01h	5 bytes	Reserved
06h	Byte	Attribute byte
07h	Byte	Drive number (0=default, 1=A:, 2=B:, etc.)
08h	8 bytes	Left-justified ASCII file name; padded with blanks
10h	3 bytes	Left-justified ASCII extension; padded with blanks
13h	Word	Current block number
15h	Word	Record size; default of 80h bytes with DOS *open* or *create* functions
17h	Dword	File size
1Bh	Word	Date created/updated
1Dh	Word	Time created/updated
1Fh	8 bytes	Reserved
27h	Byte	Current record number
28h	Dword	Random record number (if record size is less than 64 bytes, only 3 bytes used)

The DOS Functions

= **Int 20**

Terminate Program

To Call
CS   Segment address of PSP

Returns
Nothing

Comments
In addition to terminating program and freeing memory used by program, Int 20 does the following: (1) restores termination-handler vector from PSP offset 0Ah; (2) restores Ctrl-C vector from PSP offset 0Eh; (3) restores critical-error handler vector from PSP offset 12h (DOS V2.0 and later); and (4) flushes file buffers to disk (does not close FCB files). After completion of these four items, control is transferred to termination-handler address.

= **Int 21/00**

Terminate Program

To Call
AH   00h
CS   PSP segment address

Returns
Nothing

Comments

Function operationally identical to Int 20. (Refer to Int 20 *Comments* for more information.)

Int 21/01

Keyboard Input with Echo

To Call

AH   01h

Returns

AL   8-bit character data

Comments

Waits for character to be input from keyboard (STDIN), echoes character to video display (STDOUT). If character is extended ASCII character, zero is returned and another call to this function is required to return scan code of key pressed.

Int 21/02

Display Output

To Call

AH   02h
DL   8-bit character data

Returns

Nothing

Comments

Directs output to video display (STDOUT). Function will handle backspace character properly as nondestructive backspace on-screen. Ctrl-C and Ctrl-Break are handled through Int 23.

Int 21/03

DOS V1

Auxiliary Input

To Call
AH   03h

Returns
AL   8-bit input data from STDAUX

Comments
Waits for and retrieves character from first serial port (STDAUX). If either Ctrl-C or Ctrl-Break is detected, Int 23 is executed.

Int 21/04

DOS V1

Auxiliary Output

To Call
AH   04h
DL   8-bit data to output to STDAUX

Returns
Nothing

Comments
Used to send character out first serial port (STDAUX). If STDAUX is not free when output is attempted, function waits until it is. Upon detection of either a Ctrl-C or Ctrl-Break, Int 23 is invoked.

Int 21/05

DOS V1

Printer Output

To Call
AH   05h
DL   8-bit data to print to STDPRN

Returns
Nothing

Comments
Waits until printer (STDPRN) is ready and then sends a byte. Ctrl-C and Ctrl-Break are detected during this function and will cause execution of Int 23.

Int 21/06

DOS V1

Direct Console I/O

To Call
AH   06h
DL   Function requested (00h through 0FEh, character to output; FFh, input character request)

Returns
If outputting character, nothing is returned.

If inputting character:
  Zero flag set (ZF = 1) if no character is available

  Zero flag cleared (ZF = 0) if character is available
  AL   8-bit data

Comments
Inputs or outputs characters depending on the setting of

DL. This function reads characters without echo and ignores Ctrl-C and Ctrl-Break. If character is extended ASCII, zero is returned and another call to this function is required to return the scan code of the key pressed. This function cannot output an FFh character.

Int 21/07

DOS V1

Direct STDIN Input

To Call

AH   07h

Returns

AL   8-bit input data

Comments

Handles input similarly to Int 21/01, except that character is not echoed to video display and no Ctrl-C or Ctrl-Break handling is supported. If no character is ready, function waits for one to become available. When a character is available, its ASCII value is returned. If character is extended ASCII character, zero is returned and another call to this function is required to return scan code of key pressed.

Int 21/08

DOS V1

STDIN Input

To Call

AH   08h

Returns

AL   8-bit input data

Comments

Waits for and reads a character from STDIN. When a character is available, its ASCII value is returned. If character is an extended ASCII character, zero is returned and another call to this function is required to return scan code of key pressed. If either Ctrl-C or Ctrl-Break is detected, Int 23 is executed.

Int 21/09

DOS V1

Display String

To Call

AH   09h
DS:DX   Pointer to string terminated by $

Returns

Nothing

Comments

Outputs contiguous series of characters in same way Int 21/02 displays single characters. All characters beginning at specified address are output until a dollar sign ($, ASCII code 24h) is encountered.

Int 21/0A

DOS V1

Buffered STDIN Input

To Call

AH   0Ah
DS:DX   Pointer to input buffer

Returns

Nothing

Comments

Input is taken from STDIN and is placed in a user-defined buffer area. The buffer is set up as follows:

Offset	Contents
0	Maximum bytes to read
1	Number of bytes read
2–?	Actual bytes from keyboard

To use this function, store the number of bytes allowed for input in first byte of buffer pointed to by DS:DX. Realistic minimum buffer size is 2 bytes (1 byte of input plus carriage return). Max buffer size is 255.

Characters are read and placed in buffer, beginning with third byte of buffer. ASCII characters require one byte; extended ASCII characters require two (NUL followed by scan code). When actual number of characters read reaches one less than the buffer size, new characters are ignored, and bell rings with each keystroke. When Enter is pressed, number of bytes stored (not counting the carriage return) is placed in second byte of buffer.

Input allows type ahead, and all keyboard editing commands are active. Ctrl-C and Ctrl-Break functions also are active, resulting in execution of Int 23.

Int 21/0B

DOS V1

Check STDIN Status

To Call

AH   0Bh

Returns

AL   00h, character not available

FFh, character available

Comments

Checks whether character is available from STDIN
(normally the keyboard). An actual character is not
returned by this function, which merely provides an
indication of availability. If Ctrl-C or Ctrl-Break is
detected, Int 23 is invoked.

Int 21/0C

DOS V1

Clear Buffer and Input

To Call

| AH | 0Ch |
| AL | DOS input function to perform (01h, 06h, 07h, 08h, or 0Ah) |

Returns

Return defined by function invoked through AL

Comments

An alternative entry point for other DOS input functions. The only operation performed by this function is
to clear the input buffer; then control is passed to DOS
function requested in AL. Calling and return values and
programming considerations of these other DOS input
functions apply (see appropriate DOS Int 21 functions).

Int 21/0D

DOS V1

Reset Disk

To Call

| AH | 0Dh |

Returns

Nothing

Comments

Writes contents of disk buffers to their corresponding disk files (flushes disk buffers). Does not update disk directory and should not be used in place of a file-close operation.

Int 21/0E

Select Disk

To Call

AH	0Eh
DL	Drive number (A: = 0 through Z: = 25)

Returns

AL	Last drive number (A: = 1 through Z: = 26)

Comments

Sets default drive and returns number of logical drives (block-oriented devices) installed. Beginning with DOS V3, function returns a minimum last drive value equal to the number of logical drives, the LASTDRIVE value from CONFIG.SYS file, or 5 (default for LAST-DRIVE), whichever is greater.

Int 21/0F

Open File (FCB)

To Call

AH	0Fh
DS:DX	Pointer to unopened FCB

Returns

AL   00h, File opened successfully

               FFh, File not opened

Comments

Used to open existing disk file using an FCB. This function will not create a file (see Int 21/16). Function is called after filling in drive, file name, and extension fields of FCB. Drive designations are 0 (default drive), 1 (A:), 2 (B:), etc. Function sets FCB block field to zero; record size to 80h; and file size, date, and time from requested file's directory entry.

Int 21/10

DOS V1

Close File (FCB)

To Call

AH   10h

DS:DX   Pointer to opened FCB

Returns

AL   00h, File closed successfully

              FFh, File not closed

Comments

Used to close a previously opened disk file that uses an FCB. This function is essential with FCB files because it forces DOS to update file's directory entry. To use function, provide the information in FCB's file-name, extension, and drive-designator fields.

Int 21/11

DOS V1

Search for First Entry (FCB)

To Call
AH	11h
DS:DX	Pointer to unopened FCB

Returns
AL	00h, Match was found
	FFh, No match was found

Comments

Used to search for first occurrence of specified directory entry. To use this function, provide the file name, extension, and drive designators in the appropriate FCB fields. Beginning with DOS V2.1, the question mark (?) is supported as a wild card. Asterisks (*) are allowed as wild cards only under DOS V3.

Use an extended FCB to search for a file with a specific attribute. Valid attributes are derived from the attribute bit settings and include the following:

Value	File types matched
00h	Normal
02h	Normal and hidden
04h	Normal and system
06h	Normal, hidden, and system
08h	Volume labels
10h	Directories

Upon successful completion, the DTA holds an unopened FCB for the file that was found. If search is called with an extended FCB, DTA has extended FCB. If you are using wild-card characters to search for files, and no error was returned from this function, you can continue searching by using Int 21/12.

Int 21/12

DOS V1

Search for Next Entry (FCB)

To Call

AH	12h
DS:DX	Pointer to FCB returned by Int 21/11 or 21/12

Returns

AL	00h, Match found
	FFh, No match found

Comments

Continues a directory search begun with Int 21/11. Can be called as many times as necessary to locate a given file within directory, but will search only for next matching entry, not first entry. FCB pointed to by DS:DX should be the same one used in previous search.

When successfully completed, the DTA holds an un-opened FCB for the file found. If search was initiated with extended FCB, DTA will have extended FCB.

Int 21/13

DOS V1

Delete File (FCB)

To Call

AH	13h
DS:DX	Pointer to unopened FCB

Returns

AL	00h, File deleted
	FFh, File not deleted

Comments

Used to delete normal files using an FCB. Read-only files, system files, hidden files, volume labels, or directories cannot be deleted with this function.

To use, provide the file name, extension, and drive designators in the appropriate FCB fields. Beginning with DOS V2.1, a question mark (?), and with DOS V3, an asterisk (*) are allowed as wild cards. Do not try to delete an open file.

Int 21/14

Read Sequential File (FCB)

To Call

AH   14h

DS:DX   Pointer to opened FCB

Returns

AL   00h, Read was successful

         01h, No read, already at EOF

         02h, Read canceled, DTA boundary error

         03h, Partial read, now at EOF

Comments

Int 21/14 facilitates sequential reading of information from a disk file using an FCB. You can read information only from previously opened files (Int 21/0F).

To use, point DS:DX to an FCB created after file was opened. Reads are controlled by parameters set in the FCB. Length of read is given in record-size field. Location is given by current block and record numbers.

When complete, information read from the disk is placed in the DTA, and record address in the FCB is automatically incremented.

Int 21/15

Write Sequential File (FCB)

To Call

AH	15h
DS:DX	Pointer to opened FCB

Returns

AL	00h, Write successful
	01h, No write, disk full or read-only
	02h, Write canceled, DTA boundary error

Comments

This function allows sequential writing of data to a file using an FCB. You can write data only to a previously opened (Int 21/0F) or created (Int 21/16) file.

To use, point DS:DX to an FCB created after a file was opened or created. Parameters set in FCB control writes. Length of write is given in record-size field. Location is given by current block and record numbers.

Int 21/16

DOS V1

Create File (FCB)

To Call

AH	16h
DS:DX	Pointer to unopened FCB

Returns

AL	00h, File created
	FFh, File not created

Comments

Creates specified file and leaves it open for subsequent use with an FCB. To use, the FCB's drive, file-name, and extension fields must be provided. When you use an extended FCB, you also can assign an attribute to create a hidden file or a volume label.

Int 21/17

Rename File (FCB)

To Call

AH	17h
DS:DX	Pointer to modified FCB

Returns

AL	00h, File renamed
	FFh, File not renamed

Comments

Allows you to change name of existing disk files using a modified FCB. Only normal files can be renamed. The modified FCB has the following format:

Offset	Meaning
00h	Drive designation
01h	Original file name
09h	Original file extension
11h	New file name
19h	New file extension

Beginning with DOS V2.1, the question mark (?), and with DOS V3, the asterisk (*) are allowed as wild cards. Because file names in any given directory must be unique, this function will return an error if asked to rename a file to a name that already exists.

Int 21/19

Get Default Drive

To Call

AH	19h

Returns

AL   Current drive number (A: = 0, Z: = 25)

Comments

Used to determine which disk drive DOS is using as the
default drive.

Int 21/1A

DOS V1

Set DTA Address

To Call

AH   1Ah
DS:DX   Pointer to new DTA

Returns

Nothing

Comments

Used to specify the Disk Transfer Address to be used
by DOS. When a program is started, a default DTA of
128 bytes is set aside at offset 80h in the PSP.

Int 21/1B

DOS V1

Get Allocation Table Information

To Call

AH   1Bh

Returns

AL   Sectors per cluster
CX   Bytes per physical sector
DX   Clusters per disk
DS:BX   Pointer to media descriptor byte

Comments

Returns information basic to knowledge of capacity of disk in default drive. Beginning with DOS V2, DS:BX points to media descriptor byte, contained within the FAT, but on DOS V1 it points to the FAT in memory. Media descriptor (or FAT ID) byte can be used to identify media's formatting from following table:

Value	*Meaning*
F0h	Not identifiable
F8h	Fixed disk
F9h	Double sided, 15 sectors per track (1.2M)
F9h	Double sided, 9 sectors per track (720K)
FCh	Single sided, 9 sectors per track
FDh	Double sided, 9 sectors per track (360K)
FEh	Single sided, 8 sectors per track
FFh	Double sided, 8 sectors per track

Int 21/1C

DOS V2

Get Allocation Table Information for Specific Drive

To Call

AH	1Ch
DL	Drive number (Current drive = 0, A: = 1 through Z: = 26)

Returns

AL	Sectors per cluster
CX	Bytes per physical sector
DX	Clusters per disk
DS:BX	Pointer to media descriptor byte

Comments

Returns same information as Int 21/1B, but for the drive designated in DL.

Int 21/21

DOS V1

Random File Read (FCB)

To Call

AH   21h
DS:DX   Pointer to open FCB

Returns

AL   00h, Read successful
          01h, No read, EOF encountered
          02h, Read canceled, DTA boundary error
          03h, Partial read, EOF encountered

Comments

Facilitates reading of random (nonsequential) information from disk with an FCB. You can read information
only from a file that has been previously opened.

To use, point DS:DX at the FCB created after the file
was opened. Reads are controlled by parameters set in
the FCB. Record to read is specified by random-record
field; amount of data, by record-size field.

When complete, the FCB current position field is not
updated, but information read from disk is in the DTA.

Int 21/22

DOS V1

Random File Write (FCB)

To Call

AH   22h
DS:DX   Pointer to open FCB

Returns

AL   00h, Write successful
          01h, No write, disk full or read-only

02h, Write canceled, DTA boundary error

Comments

Facilitates writing of nonsequential information from the DTA to disk using an FCB. You can write information only to previously opened or created files.

To use, point DS:DX at the FCB created after the file was opened or created. Parameters set in FCB control writes. Record to write is specified by random-record field; amount of data, by record-size field. This function does not update FCB current position field.

Int 21/23

DOS V1

Get File Size (FCB)

To Call

AH	23h
DS:DX	Pointer to unopened FCB

Returns

AL	00h, Successful; no error
	FFh, No matching file found

Comments

Used to determine number of records in specified file through use of an FCB. File should be unopened when using this function. This function can be used after FCB's drive, file-name, extension, and record-size fields are filled in. Supplied file name must be complete and unique; wild-card characters not allowed.

If a file is located that matches specified file name, random-record field of FCB pointed to by DS:DX is updated to indicate number of records in file.

Int 21/24

DOS V1

Set Random-Record Field (FCB)

To Call
AH   24h
DS:DX   Pointer to open FCB

Returns
Nothing

Comments
Modifies an open FCB to prepare it for random-access functions. Function can be used after FCB's record-size, record-number, and block-number fields are filled in. Function modifies random-record field based on these field values. Primarily used to switch from sequential to random file I/O.

Int 21/25

DOS V1

Set Interrupt Vector

To Call
AH   25h
AL   Interrupt number
DS:DX   Pointer to new interrupt handler

Returns
Nothing

Comments
This function guarantees safe update of interrupt vector table to an address you supply. This is the only approved method of altering interrupt vectors.

Int 21/26

DOS V1

Create PSP

To Call

AH	26h
DX	Segment address for new PSP

Returns

Nothing

Comments

Copies current program's PSP at specified segment address and appropriately updates memory allocation information.

Int 21/27

DOS V1

Random Block Read (FCB)

To Call

AH	27h
CX	Number of records to read
DS:DX	Pointer to opened FCB

Returns

AL	00h, All records read successfully
	01h, No read, EOF encountered
	02h, Read canceled, DTA boundary error
	03h, Partial record read, EOF encountered
CX	Number of records read

Comments

Facilitates reading a group of consecutive random records from disk using an FCB. You can read information only from a file that has been previously opened.

Parameters in FCB control reads. Beginning record to read is specified by the random-record field; size of each record, by record-size field.

When complete, information read from disk is in DTA. When successfully completed, random record, current block, and current record fields of FCB are updated.

Int 21/28

DOS V1

Random Block Write (FCB)

To Call

AH	28h
CX	Number of records to write
DS:DX	Pointer to opened FCB

Returns

AL	00h, All records successfully written
	01h, No write, disk full or read-only
	02h, Write canceled, DTA boundary error
CX	Number of records written

Comments

Facilitates writing a group of consecutive random records from the DTA to disk using an FCB. You can write only to a previously opened or created file. Beginning record to write is specified by random-record field; size of each record, by record-size field.

Upon successful completion, FCB's random-record, current-block, and current-record fields are updated.

Int 21/29

DOS V1

Parse File Name

To Call

AH	29h
AL	Parse control flag (see table in *Comments*)
DS:SI	Pointer to text string
ES:DI	Pointer to FCB

Returns

AL	00h, No wild cards encountered
	01h, Wild cards found
	FFh, Drive specifier invalid
DS:SI	Pointer to character after parsed file name
ES:DI	Pointer to updated, unopened FCB

Comments

Extracts a file name from the command lines and places it in proper FCB format for opening. To use, start with a pointer to both the file-name string and the FCB you plan to use. This FCB does not have to be in any sort of format—it can be a block of memory sufficient to hold an FCB.

Interpretation of the file name is controlled by the *parse flag* as follows:

76543210	*Meaning*
. . . . 0	Do not ignore leading separators.
. . . . 1	Ignore leading separators.
. . . . . . 0 .	Drive ID modified whether specified or not. If not specified, defaults to 0.
. . . . . . 1 .	Drive ID modified only if specified.
. . . . . 0 . .	File name modified whether specified or not. If not specified, set to blanks.
. . . . . 1 . .	File name modified only if specified.
. . . . 0 . . .	Extension modified whether specified or not. If not specified, set to blanks.
. . . . 1 . . .	Extension modified only if specified.

Separator characters in all versions of DOS include periods, commas, colons, semicolons, equal signs, plus signs, tabs, and spaces. DOS V1 also uses quotation marks, slashes, and left and right brackets.

Returns an unopened FCB for the parsed file name and a pointer to the first characters after the file name. If there is no valid file name to parse, a pointer is returned in ES:DI such that ES:DI+1 is a blank character.

Int 21/2A

DOS V1

Get System Date

To Call

| AH | 2Ah |

Returns

CX	Year (1980 through 2099)
DH	Month (1 through 12)
DL	Day (1 through 31)
AL	Day of week (0 = Sunday, 1 = Monday, etc.)
	DOS V1.1 or later

Comments

Returns system date, based on DOS's internal clock.

Int 21/2B

DOS V1

Set System Date

To Call

AH	2Bh
CX	Year (1980 through 2099)
DH	Month (1 through 12)
DL	Day (1 through 31)

Returns

| AL | 00h, Date set successfully |
| | FFh, Date invalid, not set |

Comments

Typically, only sets the date portion of DOS's internal clock, but if your computer has a CMOS clock, this function also causes its date to be set.

Int 21/2C

DOS V1

Get System Time

To Call

AH	2Ch

Returns

CH	Hour (0 through 23)
CL	Minutes (0 through 59)
DH	Seconds (0 through 59)
DL	Hundredths of seconds (0 through 99)

Comments

Gets DOS internal time, which is only as accurate as its setting. Uses the same register format as Int 21/2D.

Int 21/2D

DOS V1

Set System Time

To Call

AH	2Dh
CH	Hour (0 through 23)
CL	Minutes (0 through 59)
DH	Seconds (0 through 59)
DL	Hundredths of seconds (0 through 99)

Returns

AL   00h, Time set successfully

FFh, Time invalid, not set

Comments

Typically, only sets the time portion of DOS's internal clock, but if your computer has a CMOS clock, this function also causes its time to be set.

Int 21/2E

DOS V1

Set Verify Flag

To Call

AH   2Eh

AL   00h, Turn off verify

01h, Turn on verify

DH   00h, (DOS version earlier than 3.0)

Returns

Nothing

Comments

Turning on verify flag increases security when writing to disk and increases disk transfer time. Int 21/54 can be used to determine current setting of verify flag.

Int 21/2F

DOS V2

Get DTA Address

To Call

AH   2Fh

Returns
ES:BX   Pointer to DTA

Comments
Default DTA is 128-byte buffer at offset 80h in PSP.
Int 21/1A sets DTA; this function tells you where it is.

Int 21/30
DOS V2

Get DOS Version Number

To Call
AH   30h

Returns
AL   Major version number (2, 3, 4)
AH   Minor version number (2.1 = 10)
BX   00h
CX   00h

Comments
Returns major and minor version numbers for DOS
under which your program is running. DOS versions
earlier than V2.0 return 0 in both AL and AH.

Int 21/31
DOS V2

Terminate and Stay Resident

To Call
AH   31h
AL   Return code
DX   Memory size to reserve (in paragraphs)

Returns

Nothing

Comments

Terminates operation of program but does *not* release program's assigned memory and does not close any open files. This function allows more than 64K of memory and allows control of return code, which is available to parent program through Int 21/4D or to a batch file through the ERRORLEVEL parameter.

This function attempts to allocate memory requested in DX out of memory allocated when program was started. Memory assigned via Int 21/48 is not affected.

Int 21/33

DOS V2

Get/Set System Values

To Call

AH	33h
AL	00h, Getting flag status
AL	01h, Setting flag status
DL	00h, Ctrl-Break checking off
	01h, Ctrl-Break checking on
AL	05h, Get boot drive number (DOS V4)

Returns

If AL=0

| DL | 00h, Ctrl-Break checking off |
| | 01h, Ctrl-Break checking on |

If AL=5

| DL | Boot drive number (1=A:, 2=B:, etc.) |

Comments

Checks for system variables; either Ctrl-C or Ctrl-Break checking during Int 21 functions (return or set),

or returns drive number from which system was booted.
Returning boot drive number is new to DOS V4.

Int 21/35

DOS V2

Get Interrupt Vector

To Call
AH	35h
AL	Interrupt number

Returns
ES:BX	Pointer to interrupt handler

Comments
The only *approved* way to get current setting of
interrupt vector. Guaranteed to work cleanly and return
reliable value for vector.

Int 21/36

DOS V2

Get Free Disk Space

To Call
AH	36h
DL	Disk drive (0 = default, 1 = A:, etc.)

Returns
AX	Sectors per cluster, FFFFh if drive invalid
BX	Number of available clusters
CX	Bytes per sector
DX	Clusters on drive

Comments
This function, which is similar to Int 21/1B and 21/1C,

returns basic information that can be used to determine
available space on disk.

Int 21/38

DOS V2

Get/Set Country Information

To Call

AH	38h

Get Current Country Information

AL	00, get current country information

With DOS V3.0 and later:

AL	01–FEh specified country code <255
	FFh country code is in BX
BX	Country code if AL=FFh
DS:DX	Pointer to buffer for information

Set Current Country (DOS V3.0 and later)

AL	01–FEh specified country code <255
	FFh country code is in BX
BX	Country code if AL=FFh
DX	FFFFh

Returns

Carry flag clear if successful

BX	Country code (DOS V3 only)
DS:DX	Pointer to returned country information

Carry flag set if error

AX	02h, Invalid country (file not found)

Comments

Returns a pointer to a table containing country-specific
display information. On DOS V3 and later, function
can be used also to set country information.

The format of the country information table pointed to
by DS:DX follows:

DOS V2

Offset	Length	Meaning
00h	Word	Date and time format
		0 = USA m d y, hh:mm:ss
		1 = Europe d m y, hh:mm:ss
		2 = Japan y m d, hh:mm:ss
02h	2 bytes	ASCIIZ currency symbol
04h	2 bytes	ASCIIZ thousands separator
06h	2 bytes	ASCIIZ decimal separator
08h	18 bytes	Reserved

DOS V3

Offset	Length	Meaning
00h	Word	Date format (same as under DOS V2)
02h	5 bytes	ASCIIZ currency symbol
07h	2 bytes	ASCIIZ thousands separator
09h	2 bytes	ASCIIZ decimal separator
0Bh	2 bytes	ASCIIZ date separator
0Dh	2 bytes	ASCIIZ time separator
0Fh	Byte	Currency symbol format
		00h = symbol leads, no space
		01h = symbol follows, no space
		02h = symbol leads, one space
		03h = symbol follows, one space
		04h = replaces decimal separator
10h	Byte	Number of digits after decimal
11h	Byte	Time format
		Bit 0 = 0, 12-hour clock
		1, 24-hour clock
12h	Dword	Case map call address
16h	2 bytes	ASCIIZ data list separator
18h	10 bytes	Reserved

Int 21/39

Create Subdirectory

To Call

AH	39h
DS:DX	Pointer to ASCIIZ path specification

Returns

Carry flag clear if successful

Carry flag set if error

AX	03h, Path not found
	05h, Access denied

Comments

Allows creation of new directories. Function will return an error and not create requested directory if directory already exists, if any element of path name does not exist, or if directory is from root and root is full.

Int 21/3A

DOS V2

Remove Subdirectory

To Call

AH	3Ah
DS:DX	Pointer to ASCIIZ path specification

Returns

Carry flag clear if successful

Carry flag set if error

AX	03h, path not found
	05h, access denied
	06h, current directory
	10h, current directory

Comments

Allows deletion of a specified directory, but only if it exists, is empty, and is not the default directory.

Int 21/3B

DOS V2

Set Directory

To Call

AH	3Bh
DS:DX	Pointer to ASCIIZ path string

Returns

Carry flag clear if successful

Carry flag set if error
AX	03h, Path not found

Comments

Allows you to change the current directory (similar to DOS's CD or CHDIR commands).

Int 21/3C

DOS V2

Create/Truncate File (handle)

To Call

AH	3Ch
CX	File attribute
DS:DX	Pointer to ASCIIZ file specification

Returns

Carry flag clear if successful
AX	File handle

Carry flag set if error
AX	03h, Path not found
	04h, No handles available
	05h, Access denied

Comments

Creates and opens a specified file if it doesn't exist or, if it does exist, truncates it to zero length and opens it.

Desired file is named by an ASCIIZ string, which may contain drive and path specifiers. This function cannot be used to create subdirectories or volume labels.

═ Int 21/3D ═══════════════════════

DOS V2

Open File (handle)

To Call

AH	3Dh
AL	Access mode (DOS V2)
DS:DX	Pointer to ASCIIZ file specification (DOS V3 access and file-sharing mode)

Returns

Carry flag clear if successful
AX   File handle

Carry flag set if error
AX	01h, Invalid function
	02h, File not found
	03h, Path not found
	04h, No handles available
	05h, Access denied
	0Ch, Invalid access code

Comments

To open a file, specify the file name as an ASCIIZ string. Normal, hidden, or system files are accessible. The following table shows how to set AL for DOS V2 and V3 (only bits 0 through 2 are used in DOS V2).

76543210	*Meaning*
.....000	Read access
.....001	Write access
.....010	Read/write access
....0...	Reserved (must be 0)
.000....	Sharing mode—compatibility mode
.001....	Sharing mode—read/write access denied

76543210	_Meaning_
.010....	Sharing mode—write access denied
.011....	Sharing mode—read access denied
.100....	Sharing mode—full access permitted
0.......	Inherited by child processes
1.......	Private to current process

On successful return, file is opened for access in desired mode with read/write pointer at beginning of file. The returned file handle (16-bit number) is used to later reference the opened file.

Int 21/3E

DOS V2

Close File (handle)

To Call
AH	3Eh
BX	File handle

Returns
Carry flag clear if successful

Carry flag set if error
| AX | 06h, Invalid handle |

Comments
Used to close previously opened or created file using DOS file-handling functions. Handle is freed for later use, and any file updates are done. The file's date stamp is updated if changes are made.

Int 21/3F

DOS V2

Read File or Device (handle)

To Call

AH	3Fh
BX	File handle
CX	Number of bytes
DS:DX	Pointer to buffer area

Returns

Carry flag clear if successful

AX	Number of bytes read

Carry flag set if error

AX	05h, Access denied
	06h, Invalid handle

Comments

Transfers a designated number of bytes from disk to buffer. If successfully completed, but AX is less than CX, a partial read occurred before end of file (EOF). If EOF has already been reached when this function is called, carry flag will be set but AX will be zero.

Int 21/40

DOS V2

Write to File or Device (handle)

To Call

AH	40h
BX	File handle
CX	Number of bytes to write
DS:DX	Pointer to buffer of data to write

Returns

Carry flag clear if successful

AX	Number of bytes written

Carry flag set if error

AX	05h, Access denied
	06h, Invalid handle

Comments

Simply specify a file handle and the number of bytes, and point to the data buffer. This function then writes that number of bytes to the current position in the file.

Upon return, AX contains either the number of bytes written or an error code. Normally, the value returned in AX is the same as the number of bytes to write (CX). If the write was successful and AX is less than CX, a partial record was written.

Int 21/41

DOS V2

Delete File

To Call

AH	41h
DS:DX	Pointer to ASCIIZ file specification

Returns

Carry flag clear if successful

Carry flag set if error

AX	02h, File not found
	05h, Access denied

Comments

Deletes a file by marking directory entry with an E5h in first byte of file name. Nothing else is changed in directory entry. Clusters allocated to file are returned to system for reuse. Wild cards not allowed in file name.

Int 21/42

DOS V2

Move File Pointer

To Call

AH	42h
AL	Method code
	00h, Offset from beginning of file
	01h, Offset from current position
	02h, Offset from end of file
BX	File handle
CX:DX	Offset desired

Returns

Carry flag clear if successful
   DX:AX   New file-pointer location

Carry flag set if error
   AX   01h, Invalid function (file sharing)
          06h, Invalid handle

Comments

Adjusts file read/write pointer to a new position set from beginning, end, or current position within file.

Int 21/43

DOS V2

Get/Set File Attributes

To Call

AH	43h
AL	00, Get file attributes
	01, Set file attributes
CX	New attribute when setting (see table)
DS:DX	Pointer to ASCIIZ file specification

Returns

Carry flag clear if successful
   CX   Attribute if get (see table)

Carry flag set if error

AX	01h, Invalid function (file sharing)
	02h, File not found
	03h, Path not found
	05h, Access denied

Comments

Only the following file attributes values can be set with this function:

6543210	*Meaning*
. 1	Read only
. . . . . 1 .	Hidden
. . . . 1 . .	System
. 1	Archive

Int 21/44/00

IOCTL: Get Device Information

To Call

AH	44h
AL	00h
BX	Handle

Returns

Carry flag clear if successful

DX	Device information (see table)

Carry flag set if error

AX	01h, Invalid function
	05h, Access denied
	06h, Invalid handle

Comments

On return, DX contains coded information about character device or file referenced by file handle in BX. The codes and their meanings follow:

Character Device

FEDCBA98 76543210	*Meaning*
. . . . 1	Standard input device
. . . . 1.	Standard output device
. . . . 1..	NUL device
. . . . 1...	Clock device
. . . . x....	Reserved
. . . . 0.....	Cooked mode
. . . . 1.....	Raw (binary) mode
. . . . 0......	End of file for input
. . . . 1.......	Character device
..xxxxxx	Reserved
.1......	Processing of strings sent via sub-functions 02h and 03h is possible.
x.......	Reserved

Block Device (Disk File)

FEDCBA98 76543210	*Meaning*
. . . . xxxxxx	Drive number (0 = A:, 1 = B:, etc.)
. . . . 0......	File has been written
. . . . 0.......	Disk file
xxxxxxxx	Reserved; must be set to zero

Handle in BX must refer to an open file or device. If not, function returns error code 06h (invalid handle).

Int 21/44/01

IOCTL: Set Device Information

To Call

AH	44h
AL	01h
BX	Handle
DX	Device data word

Returns

Carry flag clear if successful

Carry flag set if error
    AX   01h, Invalid function
              05h, Access denied
              06h, Invalid handle

Comments

Allows you to set a limited portion of the device data
word for character devices only. The only bit normally
modified in this call is bit 5.

If DH is not zero, subfunction returns error code 01h.
This subfunction also requires that handle refer to an
open device. The following table gives interpretation of
the Device Data Word (DX).

FEDCBA98 76543210	Meaning
....1	Standard input device
....1.	Standard output device
....1..	NUL device
....1...	Clock device
....x....	Reserved
....0.....	Cooked mode
....1.....	Raw (binary) mode
.... .0......	End of file for input
.... 1.......	Character device
xxxxxxxx	Reserved

Int 21/44/02

DOS V2

IOCTL: Character Device Read

To Call

AH	44h
AL	02h
BX	Handle
CX	Number of bytes to get
DS:DX	Pointer to data buffer

Returns

Carry flag clear if successful

AX   Number of bytes transferred

Carry flag set if error

AX   01h, Invalid function
          05h, Access denied
          06h, Invalid handle

Comments

Arbitrary driver information can be passed through calling program in control string. Subfunction may initiate I/O to or from device, but does not necessarily have to. How driver responds to request is up to driver. Bit 14 of Subfunction 00h indicates whether driver can provide or respond to control strings.

Int 21/44/03

DOS V2

IOCTL: Character Device Write

To Call

AH   44h
AL   03h
BX   Handle
CX   Number of bytes to send
DS:DX   Pointer to data buffer

Returns

Carry flag clear if successful

AX   Number of bytes transferred

Carry flag set if error

AX   01h, Invalid function
          05h, Access denied
          06h, Invalid handle

Comments

Arbitrary information about driver can be passed to

driver in control string. Subfunction may initiate I/O to or from device, but does not have to. Bit 14 of Subfunction 00h indicates whether driver can provide or respond to control strings.

Int 21/44/04

IOCTL: Block Driver Read

To Call

AH	44h
AL	04h
BL	Drive number
CX	Number of bytes to get
DS:DX	Pointer to data buffer

Returns

Carry flag clear if successful

AX   Number of bytes transferred

Carry flag set if error

AX   01h, Invalid function
           05h, Access denied
           06h, Invalid handle

Comments

Arbitrary information about block driver can be passed from it in a control string. Subfunction may initiate I/O to or from device, but does not necessarily have to. How driver responds to request is up to driver. Block device drivers are not required to support this subfunction; if they do not, error code 01h is returned.

Int 21/44/05

IOCTL: Block Driver Write

To Call

AH	44h
AL	05h
BL	Drive number
CX	Number of bytes to send
DS:DX	Pointer to data buffer

Returns

Carry flag clear if successful

AX	Number of bytes transferred

Carry flag set if error

AX	01h, Invalid function
	05h, Access denied
	06h, Invalid handle

Comments

Arbitrary information about block driver can be passed to it in a control string. Subfunction may initiate I/O to or from device, but does not have to. Block device drivers are not required to support this subfunction.

Int 21/44/06

DOS V2

IOCTL: Get Input Status

To Call

AH	44h
AL	06h
BX	Handle

Returns

Carry flag clear if successful

AL	00h, at EOF (files) or not ready (character devices)
	FFh, not at EOF (files) or ready (character devices)

Carry flag set if error
AX   01h, Invalid function
       05h, Access denied
       06h, Invalid handle

Comments

Indicates whether a device or file is ready for input. You can test files for EOF except when positioned at EOF by Int 21/42.

Int 21/44/07

DOS V2

IOCTL: Get Output Status

To Call

AH   44h
AL   07h
BX   Handle

Returns

Carry flag clear if successful
AL   00h, Ready (files) or not ready (character devices)
       FFh, Ready (files or character devices)

Carry flag set if error
AX   01h, Invalid function
       05h, Access denied
       06h, Invalid handle

Comments

With this subfunction, you can tell whether a particular device or file is ready for an output operation. Notice that files always return *ready*; character devices do not.

Int 21/44/08

IOCTL: Block Device Removable?

To Call

AH	44h
AL	08h
BL	Drive number

Returns

Carry flag clear if successful

AX	00h, Removable media
	01h, Nonremovable media

Carry flag set if error

AX	01h, Invalid function
	0Fh, Invalid drive

Comments

With this subfunction, applications that need to locate data files or overlays on a particular device can determine whether device is removable.

Int 21/44/09

IOCTL: Block Device Local or Remote?

To Call

AH	44h
AL	09h
BL	Drive number (0=current, 1=A:, etc.)

Returns

Carry flag clear if successful

DX	Device attribute word (if bit 12 = 1, drive is remote; if 0, drive is local)

Carry flag set if error
AX   01h, Invalid function
      0Fh, Invalid drive

Comments

Determines whether a block device is local or remote.
If network has not been started, this subfunction returns
error code 01h (invalid function).

Int 21/44/0A

DOS V3.1

IOCTL: Handle Local or Remote?

To Call
AH   44h
AL   0Ah
BX   Handle

Returns

Carry flag clear if successful
DX   Device attribute word (if bit 15 = 1, handle
      is remote; if 0, handle is local)

Carry flag set if error
AX   01h, Invalid function
      06h, Invalid handle

Comments

Determines whether handle is local or remote. If
network has not been started, this subfunction returns
error code 01h (invalid function).

Int 21/44/0B

DOS V3.0

IOCTL: Set Sharing Retry Count

To Call

AH	44h
AL	0Bh
CX	Pause between retries
DX	Number of retries

Returns

Carry flag clear if successful

Carry flag set if error
  AX   01h, Invalid function

Comments

When working with multiple PCs over a network, retry parameters are associated with file-locking mechanisms. The two parameters (retry count and pause between retries) are dependent on system. Differences in CPU and clock speed have an effect on actual length of pause. Defaults are PAUSE=1 and RETRY=3.

═ Int 21/44/0C

DOS V3.2

IOCTL: Generic I/O for Handles

To Call

AH	44h
AL	0Ch
BX	Handle
CH	Category code (device type)
	05h, Printer (DOS 3.2)
	00h, Unknown (DOS 3.3)
	01h, COMx (DOS 3.3)
	03h, CON (DOS 3.3)
	05h, LPTx (DOS 3.3)
CL	Minor function code (if CH=3 or CH=5)
	45h, Set iteration count (DOS 3.2 only)
	65h, Get iteration count (DOS 3.2 only)
	4Ah, Select (DOS 3.3 and later)

4Ch, Prepare start (DOS 3.3 and later)
4Dh, Prepare end (DOS 3.3 and later)
5Fh, Set display info (DOS V4, CH=3 only)
6Ah, Query select (DOS 3.3 and later)
6Bh, Query prepare list (DOS 3.3 and later)
7Fh, Get display info (DOS V4, CH=3 only)

DS:DX   Pointer to iteration count word (DOS 3.2)
Pointer to parameter block (DOS 3.3)

Returns

Carry flag clear if successful

Carry flag set if error
AX   01h, Invalid function

Comments

Iteration count word specifies the number of times an operation will be attempted before giving up. With DOS V3.3, this subfunction was changed to handle code-page switching for devices. Use of this subfunction is beyond the scope of this quick reference.

Int 21/44/0D

DOS V3.2

IOCTL: Generic I/O for Block Devices

To Call

AH   44h
AL   0Dh
BL   Drive number
CH   Category code (device type)
08h, Disk drive (block device)
CL   Minor function code
40h, Set parameters for block device
41h, Write track on logical drive
42h, Format/verify track on logical drive
47h, Set access flag (DOS V4)
60h, Get parameters for block device

61h, Read track on logical device
62h, Verify track on logical drive
67h, Get access flag (DOS V4)

DS:DX   Pointer to parameter block

Returns

Carry flag clear if successful

Carry flag set if error

AX   01h, Invalid function
02h, Invalid drive

Comments

Extends capability to control block devices. Several primitive operations are controlled through this IOCTL call in device-independent fashion. The minor functions are beyond the scope of this quick reference.

Int 21/44/0E

DOS V3.2

IOCTL: Get Logical Drive Map

To Call

AH   44h
AL   0Eh
BL   Drive number (0=current, 1=A:, etc.)

Returns

Carry flag clear if successful

AL   Logical drive number assigned (0 = only one drive assigned; 1 = A:, 2 = B:, etc.)

Carry flag set if error

AX   01h, Invalid function
02h, Invalid drive

Comments

Drive number returned by this call tells you the last

drive designation used to access the drive if more than one logical drive designation applies to the device.

Int 21/44/0F

DOS V3.2

IOCTL: Set Logical Drive Map

To Call
AH	44h
AL	0Fh
BL	New drive number (0=current, 1=A:, etc.)

Returns
Carry flag clear if successful

AL	Drive number (0 = only one logical drive assigned; 1 = A:, 2 = B:, etc.)

Carry flag set if error

AX	01h, Invalid function
	02h, Invalid drive

Comments
Used for changing the logical drive to be accessed next through a physical drive. Upon successful return, the value in AL should equal the value in BL when calling.

Int 21/45

DOS V2

Duplicate Handle

To Call
AH	45h
BX	File handle

Returns

Carry flag clear if successful

AX   New handle

Carry flag set if error

AX   04h, No handles available

06h, Invalid handle

Comments

Duplicating a file handle provides another handle for same file. File pointers move together.

Int 21/46

DOS V2

Force Duplicate Handle

To Call

AH   46h

BX   First file handle

CX   Second file handle

Returns

Carry flag clear if successful

Carry flag set if error

AX   04h, No handles available

06h, Invalid handle

Comments

Similar to Int 21/45, this function causes two handles to refer to same file and move together. If handle in CX refers to an open file, file will be closed.

Int 21/47

DOS V2

Get Current Directory

To Call

AH	47h
DL	Drive code (0 = current, 1 = A:, etc.)
DS:SI	Pointer to 64-byte scratch buffer

Returns

Carry flag clear if successful
DS:SI Pointer to current directory path

Carry flag set if error
AX 0Fh, Invalid drive

Comments

Returns ASCIIZ string path name of current directory
without drive designator or leading backslash (\). If
directory is root directory, string returned is NUL.

Int 21/48

DOS V2

Allocate Memory

To Call

AH	48h
BX	Number of paragraphs needed

Returns

Carry flag clear if successful
AX Initial segment of allocated block

Carry flag set if error
AX 07h, Memory control blocks destroyed
    08h, Insufficient memory
BX Maximum block size available (if AX =
    08h)

Comments

Pointer is segment address of base of block (base
address is AX:0000h). If attempt to get space fails,
function returns size of largest available memory block.

Int 21/49

Release Memory

To Call

AH	49h
ES	Segment of block to be released

Returns

Carry flag clear if successful

Carry flag set if error

AX	07h, Memory control blocks destroyed
	09h, Invalid memory block address

Comments

Assumes that block of memory being freed was acquired from Int 21/48. If not, function may fail or cause unpredictable errors.

Int 21/4A

Modify Memory Allocation

To Call

AH	4Ah
BX	New requested block size in paragraphs
ES	Segment of block to be modified

Returns

Carry flag clear if successful

Carry flag set if error

AX	07h, Memory control blocks destroyed
	08h, Insufficient memory
	09h, Invalid memory block address
BX	Max block size available (if AX = 08h)

Comments

This function, frequently referred to as SETBLOCK, modifies memory block received through Int 21/48.

Int 21/4B

DOS V2

Execute Program (EXEC)

To Call

AH	4Bh
AL	00, Loading and executing a program
	03, Loading an overlay
ES:BX	Pointer to parameter block (see table)
DS:DX	Pointer to ASCIIZ file specification

Returns

Carry flag clear if successful

All registers except CS and IP are lost. SS and SP should be stored before calling.

Carry flag set if error

AX	01h, Invalid function
	02h, File not found
	05h, Access denied
	08h, Insufficient memory
	0Ah, Invalid environment
	0Bh, Invalid format

Comments

Provides for executing programs and managing overlays. When a new program (child process) has completed, originating program (parent process) regains control. Parent may receive an exit code from child if child uses a termination function that transfers return codes. Primary control for operation is parameter block pointed to by ES:BX, formatted as follows:

EXEC Function (AL = 00h)

Byte	Length	Contents
00h	Word	Segment of environment block
02h	Dword	Pointer to command tail
06h	Dword	Pointer to first FCB (offset 5Ch)
0Ah	Dword	Pointer to second FCB (offset 6Ch)

Overlay Function (AL = 03h)

Byte	Length	Contents
00h	Word	Segment of load point for overlay
02h	Word	Relocation factor to be applied to code image (.EXE files only)

The environment block is a series of ASCIIZ strings used to pass environment information to program being executed. The command tail is a single string consisting of whatever would have been typed on command line after the command to be executed. Format is a single-byte length count, followed by the string of characters and terminated with a carriage return.

═ **Int 21/4C**

DOS V2

Terminate with Return Code

To Call

AH	4Ch
AL	Return code

Returns

Nothing

Comments

The approved way to terminate a program, this function is operationally identical to Int 20. Refer to *Comments* section of Int 20 for more information.

Int 21/4D

Get Return Code

To Call
AH   4Dh

Returns
AH   System exit code
          00h = Normal termination
          01h = Termination by Ctrl-C
          02h = Termination by critical device error
          03h = Termination by call to Int 21/31
AL   Child exit code

Comments
When called, returns exit code from child process and from system once (and only once). System exit code tells you whether program terminated normally.

Int 21/4E

Search for First Match

To Call
AH   4Eh
CX   Attribute to use in search
DS:DX   Pointer to ASCIIZ file specification

Returns
Carry flag clear if successful

Carry flag set if error
AX   02h, File not found
          03h, Invalid path
          12h, No more files

Comments

When given an ASCIIZ string that contains a full file name (possibly including wild cards), this function places information about the file in the DTA. Only those files that match the attributes specified will be found. File attributes can include the following:

Value	File types matched
00h	Normal
02h	Normal and hidden
04h	Normal and system
06h	Normal, hidden, and system
08h	Volume labels
10h	Directories

When function returns, the DTA is set as follows:

Byte	Length	Contents
00h	21 bytes	Reserved for DOS
15h	Byte	Attribute of matched file
16h	Word	File time
18h	Word	File date
1Ah	Dword	File size
1Eh	13 bytes	ASCIIZ file name and extension

Int 21/4F

DOS V2

Search for Next Match

To Call

AH   4Fh

Returns

Carry flag clear if successful

Carry flag set if error
AX   12h, No more files

Comments

If wild cards are used in first search (Int 21/4E),

additional files that match wild-card specification can be found by repeatedly calling this function.

Int 21/54

Get Verify Flag

To Call
AH   54h

Returns
AL   00h, Verify off
01h, Verify on

Comments
Returns current value of read-after-write (verify) flag. Int 21/2E sets the flag.

Int 21/56

Rename File

To Call
AH   56h
DS:DX   Pointer to ASCIIZ current file name
ES:DI   Pointer to ASCIIZ new file name

Returns
Carry flag clear if successful

Carry flag set if error
AX   02h, File not found
03h, Path not found
05h, Access denied
11h, Not same device

Comments

Allows files to be renamed, even across directories. Function does not allow the use of wild cards but supports full path names. Do not rename open files, as this can cause unpredictable results.

═ Int 21/57

DOS V2

Get/Set File Date and Time

To Call

AH	57h
AL	00h, Get date and time
BX	File handle
AL	01h, Set date and time
BX	File handle
CX	Time
DX	Date

Returns

Carry flag clear if successful

CX	Time if getting date and time
DX	Date if getting date and time

Carry flag set if error

AX	01h, Invalid function (file sharing)
	06h, Invalid handle

Comments

Date and time functions work on files opened or created with the handle functions. The layout and interpretation of bits follows:

Time Field Encoding

FEDCBA98 76543210	*Meaning*
xxxxx...	Hours (0–23)
.....xxx xxx.....	Minutes (0–59)
....xxxxx	Two-second increments (0–29)

Date Field Encoding

FEDCBA98 76543210	*Meaning*
xxxxxxx.	Year − 1980
.......x xxx.....	Month (1 through 12)
....xxxxx	Day (1 through 31)

Int 21/59

DOS V3

Get Extended Error Information

To Call
AH	59h
BX	00

Returns
AX	Extended error code (see table 13)
BH	Error class (see table 14)
BL	Recommended action (see table 15)
CH	Error locus (see table 16)

Comments

Can be called after an error from any call to Int 21 or from Int 24 when an error status is returned. Also resolves an FCB function that returns an FFh. You must call this function *immediately* after an error has occurred. On return, registers CL, DX, SI, DI, BP, DS, and ES are destroyed. If there was no error, function returns AX = 0. Error information returned is shown in the following four tables.

Table 13. Extended Error Codes Returned in AX

Dec	*Hex*	*Meaning*
1	01	Invalid function
2	02	File not found
3	03	Path not found
4	04	No handles available
5	05	Access denied
6	06	Invalid handle
7	07	Memory control blocks destroyed

Dec	_Hex_	_Meaning_
8	08	Insufficient memory
9	09	Invalid memory block address
10	0A	Invalid environment
11	0B	Invalid format
12	0C	Invalid access code
13	0D	Invalid data
14	0E	Reserved
15	0F	Invalid drive
16	10	Attempt to remove current directory
17	11	Not the same device
18	12	No more files
19	13	Disk write-protected
20	14	Unknown unit
21	15	Drive not ready
22	16	Unknown command
23	17	CRC error
24	18	Bad request structure length
25	19	Seek error
26	1A	Unknown media type
27	1B	Sector not found
28	1C	Out of paper
29	1D	Write fault
30	1E	Read fault
31	1F	General failure
32	20	Sharing violation
33	21	Lock violation
34	22	Invalid disk change
35	23	FCB unavailable
36	24	Sharing buffer overflow
37	25	Reserved
38	26	Unable to complete file operation (DOS V4)
39–49	27–31	Reserved
50	32	Network request not supported
51	33	Remote computer not listening
52	34	Duplicate name on network
53	35	Network name not found
54	36	Network busy
55	37	Network device no longer exists
56	38	Net BIOS command limit exceeded

Dec	_Hex_	_Meaning_
57	39	Network adapter error
58	3A	Incorrect network response
59	3B	Unexpected network error
60	3C	Incompatible remote adapter
61	3D	Print queue full
62	3E	Not enough space for print file
63	3F	Print file deleted
64	40	Network name deleted
65	41	Access denied
66	42	Network device type incorrect
67	43	Network name not found
68	44	Network name limit exceeded
69	45	Net BIOS session limit exceeded
70	46	Temporarily paused
71	47	Network request not accepted
72	48	Print or disk redirection is paused
73–79	49–4F	Reserved
80	50	File already exists
81	51	Reserved
82	52	Cannot make directory entry
83	53	Fail on Int 24
84	54	Too many redirections
85	55	Duplicate redirection
86	56	Invalid password
87	57	Invalid parameter
88	58	Network data fault
89	59	Function not supported by network (DOS V4)
90	5A	Required system component not installed (DOS V4)

Table 14. Error Class Codes Returned in BH

Dec	_Hex_	_Meaning_
1	01	Out of resource
2	02	Temporary situation
3	03	Authorization
4	04	Internal
5	05	Hardware failure
6	06	System failure
7	07	Application program error

Dec	_Hex_	_Meaning_
8	08	Not found
9	09	Bad format
10	0A	Locked
11	0B	Media
12	0C	Already exists
13	0D	Unknown

Table 15. Recommended Action Codes Returned in BL

Code	_Meaning_
1	Retry. If not cleared in reasonable number of attempts, prompt user to Abort or Ignore.
2	Delay then retry. If not cleared in reasonable number of attempts, prompt user to Abort or Ignore.
3	Get corrected information from user (bad file name or disk drive).
4	Abort application with cleanup.
5	Abort application without cleanup (cleanup may increase problems).
6	Ignore error.
7	Prompt user to correct error and then retry.

Table 16. Error Locus Codes Returned in CH

Code	_Meaning_
1	Unknown
2	Block device (disk or disk emulator)
3	Network
4	Serial device
5	Memory related

═ Int 21/5A ═══════════════

DOS V3

Create Temporary File

***

To Call

AH	5Ah
CX	Attribute
DS:DX	Pointer to full ASCIIZ path specification

Returns

Carry flag clear if successful

AX   Handle

DS:DX   Pointer to ASCIIZ file specification with file name appended

Carry flag set if error

AX   03h, Path not found

04h, No handles available

05h, Access denied

Comments

Provide the full path name to directory (including ending backslash) where you want a temporary file created. You also can specify attribute of file you want created. The following table gives valid attributes that can be set by this function. Function returns unique file name according to its own internal rules.

Value	*File types matched*
00h	Normal
02h	Hidden
04h	System
06h	Hidden and system

Int 21/5B

DOS V3

Create File

To Call

AH   5Bh

CX   Attribute

DS:DX   Pointer to ASCIIZ file specification

Returns

Carry flag clear if successful

AX   Handle

Carry flag set if error

AX	03h, Path not found
	04h, No handles available
	05h, Access denied
	50h, File already exists

Comments

The normal method for creating a file, this function returns a file handle for later access. File is created as a normal file with read/write access. You cannot create volume labels or subdirectories. Valid attributes are the same as listed for Int 21/5A.

Int 21/5C

DOS V3

Set File Access

To Call

AH	5Ch
AL	Function code
	00h, Locking
	01h, Unlocking
BX	File handle
CX:DX	Region offset
SI:DI	Region length

Returns

Carry flag clear if successful

Carry flag set if error

AX	01h, invalid function
	06h, invalid handle
	21h, lock violation

Comments

Typically used in multitasking or networking environments to prevent collisions in file updates. Locks and unlocks must always be matched. Failure to unlock a file results in a file whose state is indeterminate.

File handles duplicated with Int 21/45 will inherit access to locked regions. Programs spawned with EXEC (Int 21/4B) do not inherit the file locks.

=Int 21/5E

DOS V3.1

Network Services

To Call

AH	5Eh
AL	00h, Get machine name
DS:DX	Pointer to buffer to receive machine name
AL	02h, Set printer setup
BX	Redirection list index
CX	Length of setup string (max of 64 bytes)
DS:SI	Pointer to setup string
AL	03h, Get printer setup
BX	Redirection list index
ES:DI	Pointer to buffer to receive setup string

Returns

Varies by subfunction

Comments

Allows control of a printer over a network. Detailed explanations of the various subfunctions are beyond the scope of this quick reference.

=Int 21/5F

DOS V3.1

Network Redirection

To Call

AH	5Fh

AL	02h, Get redirection list entry
BX	Redirection list index
DS:SI	Pointer to 128-byte buffer for device name
ES:DI	Pointer to 128-byte buffer for network name

AL	03h, Redirect device
BL	Device type
	03 = Printer
	04 = Disk drive
CX	Parameter to save for caller
DS:SI	Pointer to ASCIIZ local device name
ES:DI	Pointer to ASCIIZ network name followed by ASCIIZ password

AL	04h, Cancel redirection
DS:SI	Pointer to ASCIIZ device name

Returns

Varies by subfunction

Comments

Used to get, set, or cancel network redirection for devices (printers or disk directories) on a currently active network. COM devices, STDOUT, and STDERR cannot be redirected. Detailed explanations of the various subfunctions are beyond the scope of this quick reference.

Int 21/62

DOS V3

Get PSP Address

To Call

AH	62h

Returns

BX	Segment address of PSP

Comments

Allows the program to retrieve its PSP address at any time without having to explicitly save it.

Int 21/63

DOS V2.25 Only

Get System Lead Byte Table—gets address of system lead byte table or controls interim console flag

To Call

AH	63h
AL	Subfunction
	00h, Get address of system lead byte table
	01h, Set or clear interim console flag
	02h, Get value of interim console flag
DL	(if AL = 01)
	00h, Set interim console flag
	01h, Clear interim console flag

Returns

Subfunction 00
DS:SI	Pointer to lead byte table

Subfunction 01
  Nothing

Subfunction 02
DL	Value of interim console flag

Comments

Retrieves address of system lead byte table or allows control of interim console flag. These data structures are associated with handling 2-byte-per-character display systems such as Kanji and Hangeul. Function applies to DOS V2.25 only.

Int 21/65

DOS V3.3

Get Extended Country Information

To Call

AH	65h
AL	ID of information desired (1, 2, 4, 5, or 6)
BX	Code page of interest (-1 = current)
CX	Amount of data to return
DX	Country ID (-1 = current)
ES:DI	Pointer to buffer to return information to

Returns

Carry flag clear if successful

CX	Amount of data returned
ES:DI	Pointer to returned information buffer

Carry flag set if error

AX	01h, Invalid function
	02h, File not found

Comments

Retrieves country-specific information such as currency symbol, date format, etc.

The following tables show (by country ID, which is in parentheses in the table headings) what can be retrieved. Default (-1) represents United States. Call retrieves only as much data as specified in CX. If table contains additional data, that data will be truncated and no error will be returned.

Extended Country Information Buffer (01)

Byte	Length	Meaning
00h	Word	Info ID = 01
01h	Word	Size (38 or less)
03h	Word	Country ID
05h	Word	Code Page

For balance of table, see tables returned from Int 21/38.

Extended Country Uppercase Table (02)

Byte	*Length*	*Meaning*
00h	Byte	Info ID = 02
01h	Dword	Pointer to Uppercase Table

Extended Country File Name Uppercase Table (04)

Byte	*Length*	*Meaning*
00h	Byte	Info ID = 04
01h	Dword	Pointer to File Name Uppercase Table

Extended Country Collating Table (06)

Byte	*Length*	*Meaning*
00h	Byte	Info ID = 06
01h	Dword	Pointer to Collating Table

Int 21/66

DOS V3.3

Get/Set Global Code Page

To Call

AH	66h
AL	01h, Get global code page

AL	02h, Set global code page
BX	Active code page
DX	System code page

Returns

Carry flag clear if successful

Subfunction 01

BX	Active code page
DX	System code page

Subfunction 02
  Nothing

Carry flag set if error

AX	02h, File not found

Comments

Comments

Moves country information stored in COUNTRY.SYS into resident country buffer area, the code page.

Int 21/67

DOS V3.3

Set Handle Count

To Call

AH	67h
BX	Number of open handles to allow

Returns

Carry flag clear if successful

Carry flag set if error
   AX   Error code

Comments

Allows program to control number of file handles available for use. Memory is allocated from memory freed by Int 21/4A. If number of handles is less than current number of open files, change becomes effective when current number of files drops below new limit.

Int 21/68

DOS V3

Flush Buffer

To Call

AH	68h
BX	File handle

Returns

Carry flag clear if successful

Carry flag set if error
AX   Error code

___
Comments

Flushes DOS file buffers to disk, ensuring that all information has been securely written to the file.

Int 21/6C

Extended Open/Create

___
To Call

AH	6Ch
AL	00
BX	Open mode (see table in *Comments*)
CX	File attribute (only if creating)
DX	Function control (see table in *Comments*)
DS:SI	ASCIIZ file specification

___
Returns

Carry flag clear if successful
AX   Handle
CX   01h, File opened
            02h, File created and opened
            03h, File truncated and opened

Carry flag set if error
AX   Error code

___
Comments

An addition to the other handle open and create functions DOS provides for files. The open mode indicator (BX) is set according to the following table:

FEDCBA98 76543210	*Meaning*
....000	Read access
....001	Write access
....010	Read/write access
....0...	Reserved (must be 0)

FEDCBA98 76543210	*Meaning*
.... .000....	Sharing mode—compatibility mode
.... .001....	Sharing mode—read/write access
.... .010....	Sharing mode—write access denied
.... .011....	Sharing mode—read access denied
.... .100....	Sharing mode—full access
.... 0.......	Inherited by child processes
.... 1.......	Private to current process
...00000	Reserved
..0.....	Int 24 (critical error) functions normally for this file
..1.....	Int 24 is not generated during any file access involving this file
.0......	Write file to buffer only when internal DOS file buffer is full
.1......	Flush buffer to file after every file write (as with Int 21/68)
0.......	Reserved

The function control indicator (DX) is set as follows:

FEDCBA98 76543210	*Meaning*
....0000	If file exists, generate error and take no action
....0001	If file exists, open the file
....0010	If file exists, truncate and open
.... 0000....	If file does not exist, generate error and take no action
.... 0001....	If file does not exist, create the file
00000000	Reserved

=Int 22

DOS V1

Terminate Address

To Call
Not Applicable

Returns

Not Applicable

Comments

This is not an interrupt. It is the address to which
control is transferred when the currently executing
program ends. When a program is loaded, this address
is copied into PSP offset 0Ah. When the program
terminates, this value is restored from the PSP.

Int 23

DOS V1

Ctrl-C Interrupt Vector

To Call

Not Applicable

Returns

Not Applicable

Comments

This is not an interrupt. It is a vector that holds the
address of the routine which receives control when
Ctrl-C or Ctrl-Break detection occurs.

Int 24

DOS V1

Critical-Error Vector

To Call

Not Applicable

Returns

Not Applicable

Comments

When critical-error handler is invoked, bit 7 of AH register will be clear if problem is due to disk I/O error; otherwise bit 7 will be set. BP:SI will point to device header control block where additional information about error is stored. Registers SS, SP, DS, ES, BX, CX, and DX must be preserved by the handler.

When activated, handler should perform necessary register saves and then attempt to handle error. Only Int 21/00 through Int 21/0C can be invoked from inside a critical-error handler.

Register setup includes an error code in lower byte of DI register. These error codes, shown in the following table, are the same as those returned by the device drivers in request header:

Code	Meaning
00h	Write-protect error
01h	Unknown unit
02h	Drive not ready
03h	Unknown command
04h	Data error (bad CRC)
05h	Bad request structure length
06h	Seek error
07h	Unknown media type
08h	Sector not found
09h	Printer out of paper
0Ah	Write fault
0Bh	Read fault
0Ch	General failure

When the critical-error handler is ready to return, it should set an action code in AL:

Code	Meaning
00h	Ignore error
01h	Retry operation
02h	Terminate program through Int 23h
03h	DOS V3; fail system call in progress

Int 25

Absolute Disk Read

To Call

AL	Drive number (0 = A:, 1 = B:, etc.)
CX	Number of sectors to read or -1 if using control block address in DS:BX (DOS V4)
DX	Starting relative (logical) sector number
DS:BX	Pointer to DTA or control block (DOS V4)

Returns

Carry flag clear if successful

Carry flag set if error

AX	Error code

Comments

Reads disk sector into DTA by directly accessing the desired logical sector. Logical sectors are located starting with track 0, head 0, sector 0.

If you are using DOS 4.0 and need 32-bit sector information, set CX to -1 (FFFFh) and point DS:BX to a control block laid out as follows:

Offset	*Length*	*Meaning*
00h	Dword	Starting sector number
04h	Word	Number of sectors to read
06h	Dword	Pointer to DTA

If the carry flag is set when the function returns, AH and AL are interpreted as separate error codes. The error codes returned in AH follow; those returned in AL are the same as those returned in DI for Int 24 (see *Comments* section of Int 24).

Code	*Meaning*
80h	Attachment failed to respond
40h	Seek operation failed
20h	Controller failed
10h	Data error (bad CRC)

08h	DMA failure
04h	Requested sector not found
03h	Write-protect fault
02h	Bad address mark
01h	Bad command

This interrupt can destroy any registers except the segment registers. When function returns, flag register originally pushed on stack by Int 25 is still on the stack.

=Int 26

DOS V1

Absolute Disk Write

To Call

AL	Drive number (0 = A:, 1 = B:, etc.)
CX	Number of sectors to write or -1 if using control block address in DS:BX (DOS V4)
DX	Starting relative (logical) sector number
DS:BX	Pointer to DTA or control block (DOS V4)

Returns

Carry flag clear if successful

Carry flag set if error
| AX | Error code |

Comments

Writes disk sector from DTA by directly accessing the desired logical sector. This function is the opposite of Int 25, and operates in exactly the same fashion. The comments listed under Int 25 apply here as well.

=Int 27

DOS V1

Terminate and Stay Resident

To Call

DX	Offset of last byte plus 1 (relative to PSP) of program to remain resident
CS	Segment of PSP

Returns

Nothing

Comments

On termination, procedure restores Int 22 (Terminate Address), Int 23 (Ctrl-C Interrupt Vector), and Int 24 (Critical-Error Vector) and then transfers control to termination address. It allows program to retain its memory area (DX) so that TSR can remain active. This interrupt does not close any files that may be open.

Int 2F

DOS V3

Print Installation Check

To Call

AL	00h, Get installed status
	01h, Submit file to be printed
	02h, Remove file from print queue
	03h, Cancel all files in queue
	04h, Hold print jobs for status read
	05h, End hold for status read
DS:DX	Pointer to packet address (subfunction 01h) or ASCIIZ file specification (subfunction 02h)

Returns

Varies by subfunction

Comments

Gives a program access to printer spooler. Detailed information is beyond the scope of this quick reference. See *DOS Programmer's Reference*.

Index